# TQC SOLUTIONS

## The 14-Step Process

*Volume II*

# Applications

# TQC SOLUTIONS

## The 14-Step Process

## *Volume II*

## Applications

Edited by JUSE Problem Solving Research Group

**Productivity Press, Inc.**
Cambridge, Massachusetts    Norwalk, Connecticut

Originally published as *TQC Ni Okeru Mondai Kaiketsu Ho*, copyright © 1985 by JUSE Press, Ltd.

English translation copyright © 1991 by Productivity Press, Inc.

Productivity Press, Inc.
P.O. Box 3007
Cambridge, MA 02140
(617) 497-514

Cover Design by David B. Lennon
Typeset by Rudra Press, Cambridge, MA
Printed and bound by Arcata Graphics
Printed in the United States of America

**Library of Congress Cataloging-in-Publication Data**

TQC solutions.
    Translation of: TQC ni okeru mondai kaiketsuhō.
    Includes index.
    1. Quality control.   2. Production management.   I. Nikkagiren.   Mondai Kaiketsu Kenkyū Bukai.
TS156.T6313   1991                              658.5'62                        91-8680
ISBN 0-915299-79-8

91  92  93   10  9  8  7  6  5  4  3  2  1

# Contents

*Volume II*
*Applications*

---

**NOTE:**  Due to the format requirements of the illustrations, many of which are two-page spreads, you will occasionally find a blank page. Please note that these are intentional, and that there is no material missing from the book.

# List of Illustrations

*Volume II*

Chapter 18

# Contributors

*Committee Chairman:*

Katsuya Hosotani
    Union of Japanese Scientists and
    Engineers
    Chapters 1, 7, 9 and 17

*Committee Members:*

Tetsuhiko Ichihara
    Kajima Construction
    Chapters 3 and 10

Hideo Iwasaki
    Kinki University
    Chapters 4 (Steps 7 through 14),
    14, and 18

Kyosuki Kamijo
    Sekisui Chemical
    Chapters 13 and 16

Hiroyuki Muneshige
    Shimpu Industries
    Chapter 7

*Secretaries:*

Isao Itsukage
    Suntory
    Chapter 8

Hiroshi Matsubara
    Sumitomo Rubber
    Chapters 2 and 6

Nobuo Tabe
    Matsushita Electronic Component
    Chapter 5 and Appendix

Masakazu Yamamoto
    Yamamoto QC Office
    Chapter 4 (Steps 1 through 6)

Takashi Yamamoto
    Daihatsu Motor
    Chapters 11, 12, and 15

# TQC SOLUTIONS

## The 14-Step Process

*Volume II*

Applications

# Volume II
# Applications

Companies establish various organizations, departments, and sections to fulfill business functions. These departments and sections include research and development, product planning, design, manufacturing, and sales, among others. In TQC it is necessary to define the roles and functions of each department, to perform QC problem solving on problem areas, and to establish an excellent work system in order to economically provide goods and services that meet the needs of the customer.

In Chapters 8 through 14 we discuss effective methods of problem solving in each of these departments.

Competition between industries is growing increasingly fierce; the surrounding society is demanding more diversified, more sophisticated goods on a daily basis; and profit margins are becoming slim. One can hardly overstate the importance of new-product development in such circumstances. In this section we will discuss the seven departments that have the greatest effect on the success or failure of new-product development and quality assurance. These departments are (1) research and development, (2) product planning, (3) design, (4) production engineering, (5) manufacturing, (6) procurement, (7) sales.

We will discuss:

- the functions of the departments
- problems in the departments and ways to resolve them
- examples of effective results

We hope that this information will give the reader an understanding of how to discover and solve problems in all departments.

In Chapters 15 through 18, we examine how problem solving has been used in the TQC activities of various types of industries. At the beginning of each example we present the important points and central concepts of problem solving in that particular industry. By referring to these sections first, you will find the examples easier to understand.

Although we wanted to include examples from many types of industries, in the interest of brevity we selected the four types of industries that are the most common around us — assembly, process, construction, and service — and present one example of problem solving in each. As you have already learned from this book, the fundamental philosophies and principal processes of problem solving are independent of the type of industry or the business conditions; hence we think that even examples from other industries will be relevant to conditions in your own industry.

# 8

# Effective Problem Solving in the Research and Development Department

## THE FUNCTION OF THE RESEARCH AND DEVELOPMENT DEPARTMENT

### Developing New Products

To endure and progress, a company must continuously develop new products that adapt to the changing needs of the consumers and to the changing industrial structure. The following can be said of new-product development:

1. It is the accumulation of various technologies and the use of newly developed technologies to make products that have not previously existed — for example, the first airplane or the first television.
2. It is the improvement in qualities or characteristics of existing products or the development of new products with reduced costs through use of parts produced with newly developed technologies. Examples are the changes from propeller to jet aircraft, from vacuum tube to transistor radios.
3. It is the addition or improvement of information functions in existing products. Examples are the development of telephones that display communications tolls or of clocks that tell time verbally.
4. It is the change in product flows that results from, for example, the offering of specialty items in supermarkets and the home delivery of items that formerly had to be purchased in stores.

Each of the above four categories of new-product development is rooted in technology and in market research and development.

In the past few years, high technology, biotechnology, microelectronics, new materials development, and other advanced technologies have dramatically changed human life and society. To keep pace, companies have had to execute a quantum increase in their research and development activity.

## The Role of the Research and Development Department

Research and development, abbreviated R&D, is generally research tied to development. Although the two activities differ significantly, there is a strong relationship between them.

The word research is etymologically the union of *re* and *search*. "Re" means "to repeat" or "to go back," while "search" means "to seek." What are companies seeking? There are various possible answers: The principal one is that companies are seeking ways to use fundamental physical principles in the development of new products, and are seeking fundamental principles behind sociological phenomena.

*Development* in a company can be defined as the appropriate joining of existing knowledge with the sociological or physical phenomena that were discovered during the research stage, thus making possible the creation of new products that fill the desires of consumers.

## PROBLEM AREAS IN RESEARCH AND DEVELOPMENT, AND WAYS TO RESOLVE THEM

In companies, it is usually the product planning, marketing, and sales departments that are responsible for market research and development. This section, however, addresses the technical research and development that falls under the realm of the research and development department.

The worst thing that can happen in research and development is that the department is unable to develop new products that fulfill the desires of the consumers. Such a problem is usually caused by a flaw in the process by which developments are made. Typical examples include problems in

- research and development investments and leadership from the top
- finding research and development personnel
- the research and development policies and plans
- the selection of research and development themes

- the management of research and development
- education for the research and development department

Following are some hints for resolving such problems.

## R&D Investments and Leadership from the Top

Research and development activities are not undertaken to provide profitability tomorrow or in the immediate future. Indeed, one cannot guarantee that R&D will ever be profitable for the company. Nor is it something that can be started at the last minute once sales and profitability growth in the company have stopped and the situation has become unfavorable.

Decisions about research and development (including research and development investments) must be made by top management. Top management should be constantly evaluating changes in society and in patterns of consumer desires, and should be anticipating the effects of those changes on the company. Furthermore, top management should constantly watch the progress of relevant sciences and technologies worldwide, should establish direction and policies for the long-term growth of the company, and should be convinced of the need for research and development, addressing R&D issues assertively. The great number of top managers in the major electronics and chemical industries of our country who have come up through the technical research and development departments testifies to the value those industries place on research and development.

When top management is oriented toward technical research and development, then companies can attract excellent R&D personnel and provide education and dynamic activities for those personnel. They can also select appropriate R&D themes, establish appropriate organizations and systems, evaluate the soundness of results, and reduce the risk of R&D investments, thereby increasing their abilities to develop, manufacture, and sell the finished products in the world, and ensuring corporate growth.

## Employing R&D Project Managers[1]

The key to any activity is human resources. "The right person in the right place" is an age-old saying. Corporate management comprises many individual

[1] Murakami, "Policy Management in Technical Research Centers" *Quality*, 14 (1):77-81, 1984 (Japanese Quality Control Research Organization).

activities — purchasing, manufacturing, marketing, general affairs, financial management, and materials, to name a few. Activities that are not involved in research and development can get by even without the right person in the right place. But in research and development, the wrong person in the wrong place can mean ten years of no progress; the squandering of human, material, and financial resources; and the negation of tireless work. When this happens, not only does research and development stagnate, wasting management resources, but the company itself can fail. Excellent research and development personnel must be recruited, educated, and put to work. We believe that the best R&D personnel are those who remain attuned to the changing times and have some sense of direction. Companies that are heavily involved in research and development look for these qualities in their R&D personnel.

Because most R&D specialists have attended universities or have graduated from masters or doctoral programs, the best source of recommendations for potential recruits is probably university professors in charge of fundamental education. Although one hopes that university professors will take assertive steps to cultivate human resources while keeping in mind the future economy, when consulting with these professors, you should define the type of human resources your companies needs.

## QC EDUCATION FOR THE RESEARCH AND DEVELOPMENT DEPARTMENT[2]

When you examine the work methods and attitudes of highly effective R&D specialists, you find that they follow QC methods quite closely. This finding makes it all the more important to educate employees, especially newly hired employees, in standard quality. A sound education ensures that they will recognize the excellence of quality control philosophy, practices, and methods, will make extensive use of them on their own, and will promote quality control within the R&D Department.

---

[2] Gōshō, "Quality Control and Corporate Research and Development — Problems and Corrective Actions," *Quality*, 14 (1): 13-18, 1984 (Japanese Quality Control Research Organization).

## EXAMPLES OF PROBLEM-SOLVING ACTIVITIES IN RESEARCH AND DEVELOPMENT

### Overview of Technical Research Centers

As Figure 8-1 shows, the Research and Development Department Technical Research Centers at Komatsu Seisakusho were organized into a single department reporting to the company president.[3] Summaries of the responsibilities and characteristics of this department are given in Figures 8-2 and 8-3.

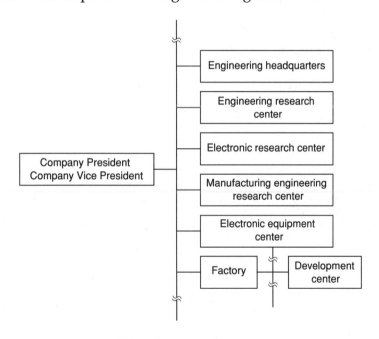

**Figure 8-1. Technical Research Centers — Organization**

1. Research of new technologies pertaining to construction equipment
2. Research of new construction equipment peripheral products and products for promising new fields

**Figure 8-2. Technical Research Centers — Responsibilities**

---

[3] This activity example is based on a report presented in 1984.

> 1. Although the research center revolves around construction equipment, recently the scope of research has extended to other fields.
>
> 2. The system management is performed systematically through the specialized technology lab, project team, and research team system.

**Figure 8-3.  Technical Research Centers — Features**

## The Policy Management (Hoshin Planning) System

*The structure of policy.* The policy (hoshin) of the Technical Research Centers comprises the long-term research direction, the long-term research plan, and the yearly policy. The objectives and critical items in achieving the yearly policies are deployed to the lower levels, and the mutual relationships and connections between the items are defined through an objective deployment chart. (See Figure 8-4.)

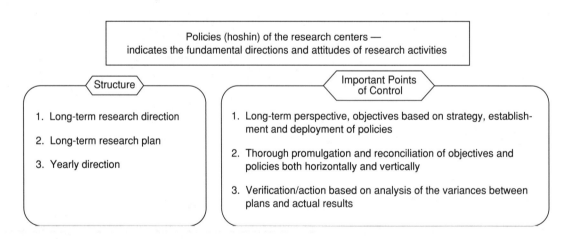

**Figure 8-4.  Technical Research Centers — Policy Management (Hoshin Planning)**

*Establishment of the long-term direction and plans.* To establish long-term direction and plans, we selected long-term research topics centered around the product planning function from the long-term objectives in the company's basic long-range plan. We then arranged these topics based on the results of studies done by the departments that would execute the research.

Then we established the long-term direction and plans at a companywide conference (through deliberations about strategy in the research committee and in the strategy study group).

Also, so that external factors such as political, economic, and technological trends, as well as internal factors such as the results of last year's activities and evaluations, would be fed back into the long-term research plan, each year we readjusted the rolling long-term research topics and objectives and reverified the yearly research topics and objectives. (See Figures 8-5 and 8-6.)

---

1. To give direction to the research activities based on a long-term perspective and strategy

2. To define important tactics in attaining long-term objectives

3. To gain both vertical and horizontal consensus about research activities on issues such as allocation of management resources

---

**Figure 8-5.  Aims of Long-term Research Directions and Plans**

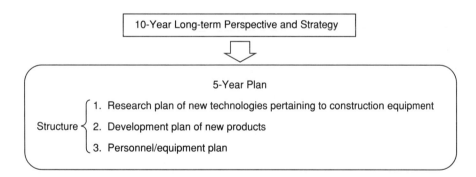

**Figure 8-6.  Structure of the Long-term Research Plan**

The system for establishing long-term research plans in the technical research centers is shown in Figure 8-7.

The long-term research plan consists of the new technology research plan (plans for researching technologies pertaining to the chief products of the company, construction equipment), new-product research and development plans, and personnel and equipment plans. Although the long-term plans are 5-year plans, they are based on the 10-year perspective and strategy.

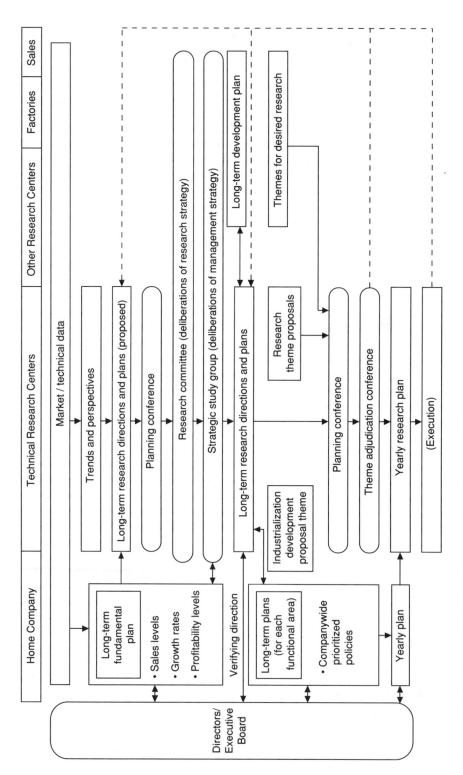

**Figure 8-7. System to Establish the Long-term Research Plan**

Although the long-term directions and plans are based on the system shown in Figure 8-4, in the process of constructing the directions and plans, the strengths and weaknesses of the company and the problems in adapting to the market are defined through discussions with related departments. These discussions narrow down the possible corrective actions and elicit a vertical and horizontal consensus about resource allocation priorities and similar issues. Furthermore, they bring about detailed studies of the coordination and correspondence of the company's long-term plans.

*Formulation of yearly policies.* In this company, the proposal for the company president's policy (hoshin) is formulated chiefly by the president's office. It passes through companywide deliberations and discussions in the separate functional areas and departments, and by the middle of November each year the next year's company president's policy is established and circulated.

In the Technical Research Centers, basic proposals for yearly hoshin are based on a combination of the company president's policy, evaluations of the results of last year's activities, topics relevant to the current year, and the new environmental conditions. Priority action items are identified (to be performed mostly by the manager's office), and results of studies by all departments in the research center and the relationships of these results to the long-term company objectives are considered.

The proposed activity plans for all of the departments in the research center are adjusted and coordinated (based upon the proposed hoshin) by a TQC committee comprising representatives of all departments. The proposals pass through the companywide review board and are presented to all employees of the Technical Research Centers on 1 January of each year. (See Figure 8-8.)

The content of the policies and directions of the Technical Research Centers includes objectives and plans. Because the process by which the hoshin are established is important, in 1980 we created a policy establishment check sheet (such as that in Figure 8-9) and have been using it since that time.

*Execution, verification, and evaluation of yearly policies and directions (do, check, action).* The policy deployment system in the Technical Research Centers is shown in Figure 8-10. Among the important measures of the yearly policy and directions are deployment into the research plans and work improvement (kaizen) plans of the offices, sections, and teams. The activities are regularly monitored through various levels of control points.

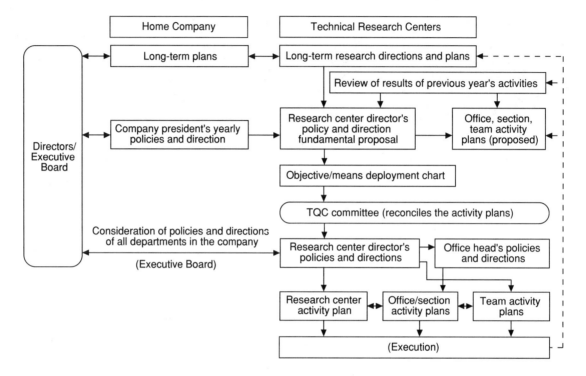

**Figure 8-8. System to Establish Yearly Policies and Directions**

1. Are there strong connections between long-term research policies and plans?
2. Is there feedback from the previous year?
3. Is there sufficient extraction and analysis of problem areas?

]...[

8. Is there coordination and reconciliation vertically and horizontally?
9. Are the plans and the budgets reconciled?
10. Are each of the items expressed clearly?

**Figure 8-9. Checkpoints for Policy (Hoshin) Establishment (Examples)**

The progress of primary action items is verified through the diagnoses of the company president (once a year), and the Technical Research Center's director (twice a year), and the results are fed back into the policies and the activity plans for the next period.

We have been performing supplemental work diagnoses since 1979, and we also use a TQC performance level evaluation system. We do this with the

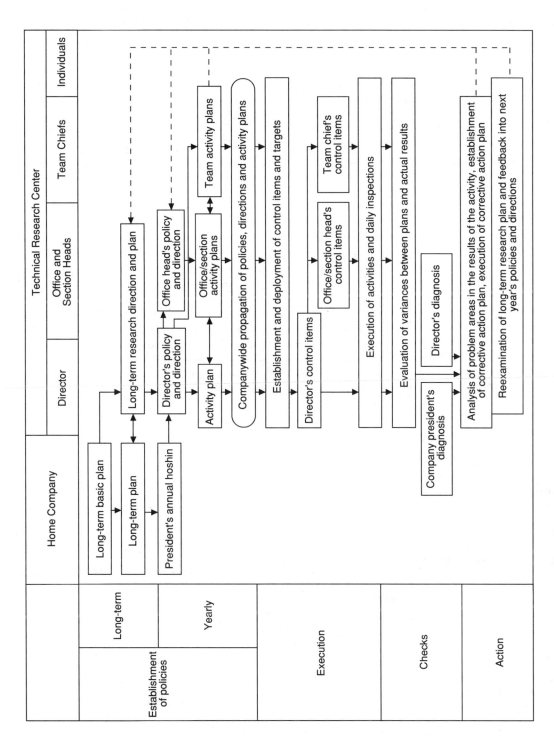

**Figure 8-10. Policy Deployment System**

intent of providing each office and each department feedback on the progress of the control activities; each functional area performs in-depth evaluations of its control methods in order to extract problems, and the results are fed back into the next period's policies and activity plans. The evaluation items compiled were based upon the Deming Prize/Implementation Prize Checklist, which we divided into two parts: One part is based on inquiries (the inquiry diagnosis) and the other part shows indexes. Each part has a five-level evaluation for each function. The objectives for each section are shown in Figures 8-11 and 8-12.

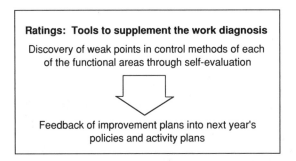

**Figure 8-11.  Aim of TQC Level Evaluation**

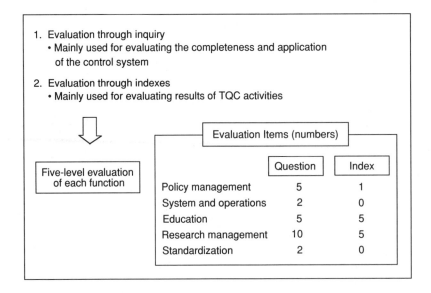

**Figure 8-12.  Detail of TQC Level Evaluation**

## Research Management and Fulfillment of Hoshin

One of the most important functions in fulfilling hoshin is research management. Research management is conducted to fulfill long-term research objectives; it induces researchers to show initiative and creativity, and it uses limited resources to optimize results. (See Figure 8-13.)

1. Plans research from a long-term perspective
2. Remains flexible to the needs of the research
3. Evaluates research and encourages researchers at every step of research

**Figure 8-13. Characteristics of Research Management Needed to Fulfill Policies and Direction**

In the Technical Research Centers, research activities are divided into three phases, and management is performed according to the objective of the research. Figure 8-14 shows the series of steps from research planning to the transfer and use of the research results. Until the feasibility of the idea is verified (phase 1 research), the researchers must be allowed to use the budget flexibly, to conceive ideas freely, and to cultivate the growth of creative ideas. Closer to the development stage, (phase 2 research), management by quality, cost, and delivery (Q, C, D) objectives is executed in detail.

*New technology development and research planning.* The timely development of products with technological features is necessary in order to adapt to the worldwide need to conserve resources and energy and to continue the long-term expansion of the company in an increasingly competitive marketplace.

To develop such products, companies must rapidly adapt to technical trends and changes, must research and develop new technologies while taking into account the needs of the market, and must transfer the results accurately to new product planning and design.

Work in the Technical Research Center begins with the awareness that the research planning activities, which range from grasping user needs to selecting research themes, are of the utmost importance. We devise the research theme plan according to the flow of Figure 8-15, understanding the qualities

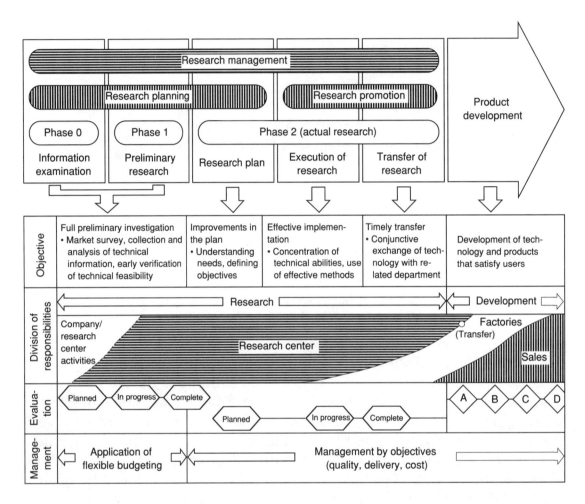

**Figure 8-14. Steps in Research Management and Their Objectives**

demanded by the market through analysis of the implementation system, identifying key problems through function deployment, evaluating ideas through technology deployment, and so forth. This is done in cooperation with involved departments.

*Carrying on and evaluating the research.* An overview of the research management system in the Technical Research Centers is shown in Figures 8-16 and 8-17. The management of the research theme activities, which were planned on the basis of long-term technological trends and perspectives, is facilitated through the use of control methods, a full preliminary study, and the cooperation of involved departments.

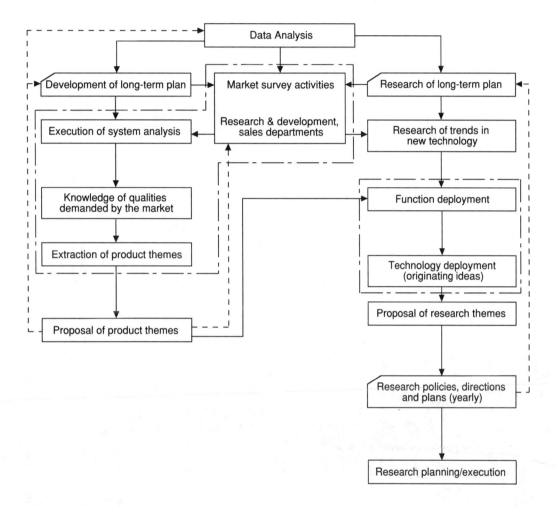

**Figure 8-15. The Flow of Research Planning**

New-product research, especially in the research stage near the beginning of the development process (phase 2 research) should be run with the cooperation of the factories, the sales departments, and the staff of the home company. The planning, in-process, and completion stages are evaluated by a companywide research evaluation committee, which discovers the problem areas, ensures corrective actions, and directs the transfer of the results to the next stage.

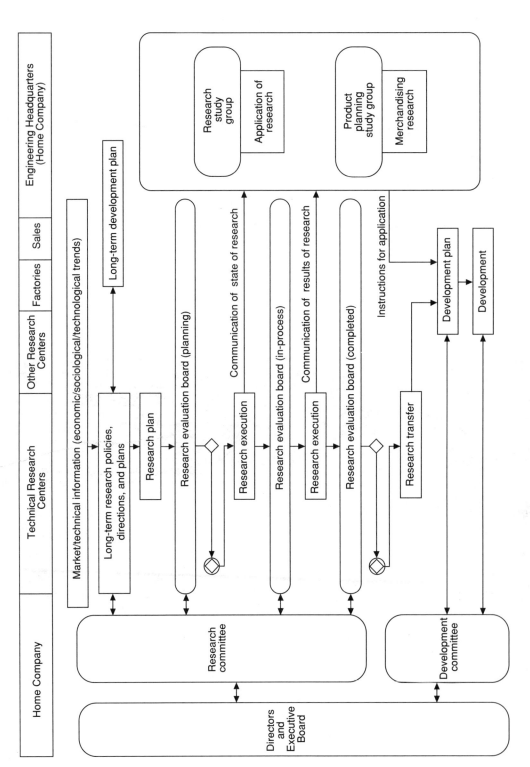

**Figure 8-16.  The Research Management System (Phase 2 Research — Researching New Technologies in Construction Equipment)**

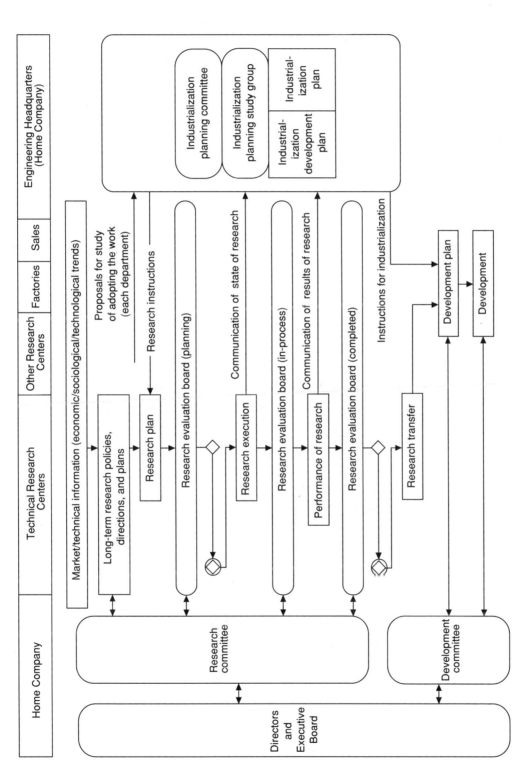

**Figure 8-17. The Research Management System (Phase 2 Research — Developing Products for New Markets)**

# 9

# Effective Problem Solving in the Product Planning Department

If the company is to grow from year to year and ensure substantial profitability, it must develop new and compelling products one after another and with proper timing. The current mainstay products will eventually become obsolete. In this era of sweeping technical revolutions, the competitive and earning powers of any product are only transient phenomena. Nevertheless, a company cannot cease to invest in research and development, pioneer new markets, or develop new products that bring high profitability.

However, there are too many cases in which companies have invested vast sums of money into research and development and missed the target altogether, creating products that don't sell and threatening the existence of the company — all because they developed new products solely according to the opinions of the engineering and manufacturing departments, without consulting other parties.

The product planning department plays a major role in the development of new products. It is no exaggeration to say that a company's survival depends largely on the skill of its product planning department. Below we discuss how to use QC problem-solving methods in new-product development departments.

## THE FUNCTION OF THE PRODUCT PLANNING DEPARTMENT

In the past, if a Japanese company had a clear manufacturing objective — whether it was televisions or automobiles — it could be satisfied to efficiently manufacture products that had already proven themselves in the American and European markets. It is not too much to say that Japan's rise to economic power was won by its strength in production technology.

21

Today, however, when there is an abundance of consumer goods available, the greatest topic facing a company is "what to make."

*Product planning* is corporate decision making on "what product, what market, what price, and in what amounts." This corresponds to the P (plan) in the PDCA cycle.

The functions of the product development department include:

1. Collecting and analyzing market data
2. Drafting and planning new products
3. Drafting and planning products for new fields
4. Performing market surveys for new-product development
5. Drafting long- and mid-term sales and profitability plans

## PROBLEM AREAS IN THE PRODUCT PLANNING DEPARTMENT

The product planning department plays the following roles:

1. It analyzes market data to extract themes for hit products that expand demand and increase market share.
2. It plans for the leading development of products whose features receive the highest rankings in customer evaluations.
3. It reconciles quality with technology and costs in the planning stage of development, to develop compelling new products.

When the product planning system is not adequate, many problems can occur, of which the following are examples:

1. Creativity and control of information are inadequate to allow the company to quickly develop innovative products and be first with them to market.
2. Access to research instruments both within and outside of the company is limited, and there is no management system for basic research.
3. There are no criteria for evaluating ideas and information.
4. The product planning evaluation system is inadequate.
5. There is no clear policy or direction for new-product development.
6. New-product development is slow.

7. The timing of new-product development is poor.
8. There is no success in abolishing old products.
9. The new-product development quality assurance system is inadequate.
10. The control of early-stage new-product flow is poor, and control when beginning mass production and repercussions in the market are not understood.

A relations diagram of the problem areas in product planning is given in Figure 9-1.

## THE METHOD OF SOLVING PROBLEMS IN THE PRODUCT PLANNING DEPARTMENT

### The Categories of New Products

Although there are many things a company must do to exercise quality control, it is especially important to plan products for which there will be a demand. If the product plan is flawed, the product produced will not be marketable no matter how efficiently the quality control activities are carried out.

There are several ways to categorize new products, as is shown in Tables 9-1 through 9-4.

### The Product Planning System

To ensure complete product planning, it is necessary to construct a product planning system and to run it properly. The following steps are usually performed:

1. Establish the targeted needs
2. Establish the target market
3. Establish the product development theme and the specifications for use
4. Determine how to fulfill the needs and specifications
5. Determine the product development theme and the specifications for use
6. Determine the basic specifications in the quality design

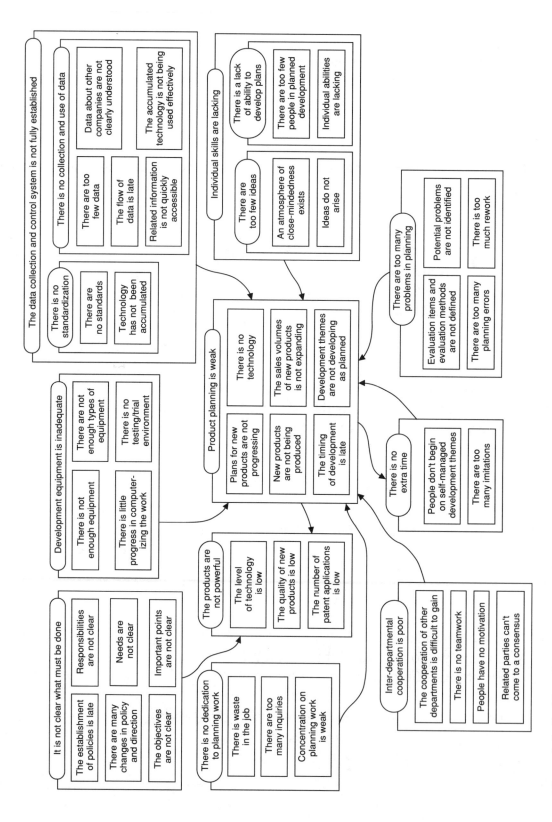

**Figure 9-1. Problem Areas in Product Planning**

**Table 9-1. Categories of New Products (1)**

| Category | Type of New Product | Technology | Application | Change in Demand | Homogenous Production |
|----------|--------------------|-----------|------------|-----------------|----------------------|
| A | New technology, new market products | New technology | New application | Causes of change | Does not stop production |
| B | New technology enhanced product | " | No new application | Does not cause a change | " |
| C | New technology substitute product | " | " | " | Stops production |
| D | New market product | Uses existing technology | New application | Causes a change | Does not stop production |
| E | Enhanced product | " | No new application | Does not cause a change | " |
| F | Substitute product | " | " | " | Stops production |

**Table 9-2. Categories of New Products (2)**

| Category | Type of New Product |
|----------|--------------------|
| A | New products based on new concepts |
| B | Development of new operations through the combination of existing products |
| C | Improvements in existing products or in their characteristics |
| D | Development of new applications for existing products |
| E | Production of a previously existent product for new markets |

7. Determine the fundamental specifications in the manufacturing design
8. Determine the marketing plan
9. Determine the target cost

Steps 1 through 5 make up the product conceptualization stage, while steps 1 through 6 make up the product planning stage. Figure 9-2 shows these steps broken down further and put together in a system.

It is important to have complete methods, tools, and documents for system management, to have a set of management rules (standards and specifications), and to ensure a smooth transition between the various steps.

**Table 9-3.  Categories of New Products (3)**

| Category | Type of New Product |
|---|---|
| A | A product based on new design principles, never before manufactured in the company |
| B | Products that through new materials, components, construction, or processes:<br>• have superior characteristics, or<br>• have expanded into new applications |
| C | Products that have been partially modified in terms of materials, parts, construction, processes, etc., improve problem areas in previously existing products |
| D | Individual products within a product line that have been partially modified to adapt to specific applications |

**Table 9-4.  Categories of New Products (4)**

| Category | Type of New Product |
|---|---|
| A | • A product that is a completely new concept anywhere in the world<br>• A product that is completely new domestically<br>• A product that is completely new to the company |
| B | • A product whose characteristics and functions have been significantly modified.<br>• A product that, although not handled by the company, could be easily merchandised in existing product fields |
| C | • An existing product with new manufacturing systems<br>• A product that is an upgrade of a formal product line and has special applications and characteristics |
| D | • A product that has improved problem areas in previous products<br>• A model change improving previous products |

## Creating the New-Product Plan Report

It is said that life is a drama. The same is true of products. Product plans should have a good story line and be properly nurtured.

We recommend that the following questions be used as guidelines when devising the product planning "story."

1. What sort of product will we make, and what will be the quality characteristics of the product?

2. When will the product be sold?
3. What will the price be?
4. What sales methods and sales channels will be used?
5. What will the sales points be?
6. What will its popular or brand name be?
7. How will it be unveiled?
8. What will the system be for increasing production when production is started?
9. Has the reaction of competitors been anticipated?
10. Has a countermeasure to resist the competitors' reaction been established?
11. How could the inventory of existing products best be dealt with?
12. What sort of latent power does the product have to resist a drop in sales levels or profitability?
13. When will the product life cycle come to an end?
14. Has a skillful way to tie it to the next new product been thought of?

Most manufacturers give careful consideration to questions 1 through 8 but we recommend that particular attention be paid to questions 9 through 14. To increase profits continuously, a company must skillfully combine existing products with their successors, and must create a product planning procedure that is compounding, comprehensive, and continuing.

The above details are normally included in the "new-product plan report."

## Important Points in Product Planning

It is important to follow the *10 points of product planning* to stimulate new demands through consumer orientation.

1. Fully establish a market data collection system, systematically and assertively collect data, analyze needs, and feed results back into product plans.
2. Adequately understand how the products are used and in what environment they are used.
3. Delve into the needs and characteristic levels of market demands and clearly identify yet-to-be-developed technologies and bottleneck engineering areas.

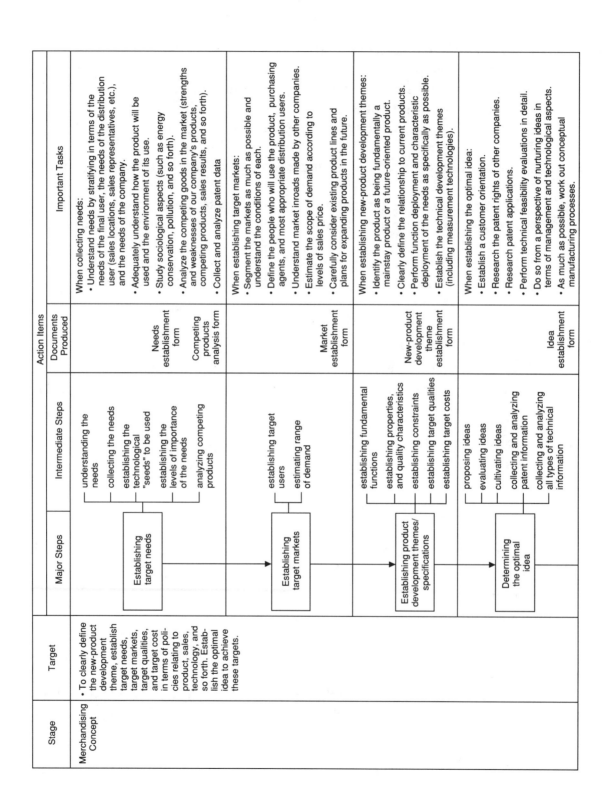

| Stage | Target | Major Steps | Intermediate Steps | Action Items — Documents Produced | Action Items — Important Tasks |
|---|---|---|---|---|---|
| Merchandising Concept | • To clearly define the new-product development theme, establish target needs, target markets, target qualities, and target cost in terms of policies relating to product, sales, technology, and so forth. Establish the optimal idea to achieve these targets. | Establishing target needs | understanding the needs<br>collecting the needs<br>establishing the technological "seeds" to be used<br>establishing the levels of importance of the needs<br>analyzing competing products | Needs establishment form<br><br>Competing products analysis form | When collecting needs:<br>• Understand needs by stratifying in terms of the needs of the final user, the needs of the distribution user (sales locations, sales representatives, etc.), and the needs of the company.<br>• Adequately understand how the product will be used and the environment of its use.<br>• Study sociological aspects (such as energy conservation, pollution, and so forth).<br>• Analyze the competing goods in the market (strengths and weaknesses of our company's products, competing products, sales results, and so forth).<br>• Collect and analyze patent data |
| | | Establishing target markets | establishing target users<br>estimating range of demand | Market establishment form | When establishing target markets:<br>• Segment the markets as much as possible and understand the conditions of each.<br>• Define the people who will use the product, purchasing agents, and most appropriate distribution users.<br>• Understand market inroads made by other companies.<br>• Estimate the scope of demand according to levels of sales price.<br>• Carefully consider existing product lines and plans for expanding products in the future. |
| | | Establishing product development themes/ specifications | establishing fundamental functions<br>establishing properties, and quality characteristics<br>establishing constraints<br>establishing target qualities<br>establishing target costs | New-product development theme establishment form | When establishing new-product development themes:<br>• Identify the product as being fundamentally a mainstay product or a future-oriented product.<br>• Clearly define the relationship to current products.<br>• Perform function deployment and characteristic deployment of the needs as specifically as possible.<br>• Establish the technical development themes (including measurement technologies). |
| | | Determining the optimal idea | proposing ideas<br>evaluating ideas<br>cultivating ideas<br>collecting and analyzing patent information<br>collecting and analyzing all types of technical information | Idea establishment form | When establishing the optimal idea:<br>• Establish a customer orientation.<br>• Research the patent rights of other companies.<br>• Research patent applications.<br>• Perform technical feasibility evaluations in detail.<br>• Do so from a perspective of nurturing ideas in terms of management and technological aspects.<br>• As much as possible, work out conceptual manufacturing processes. |

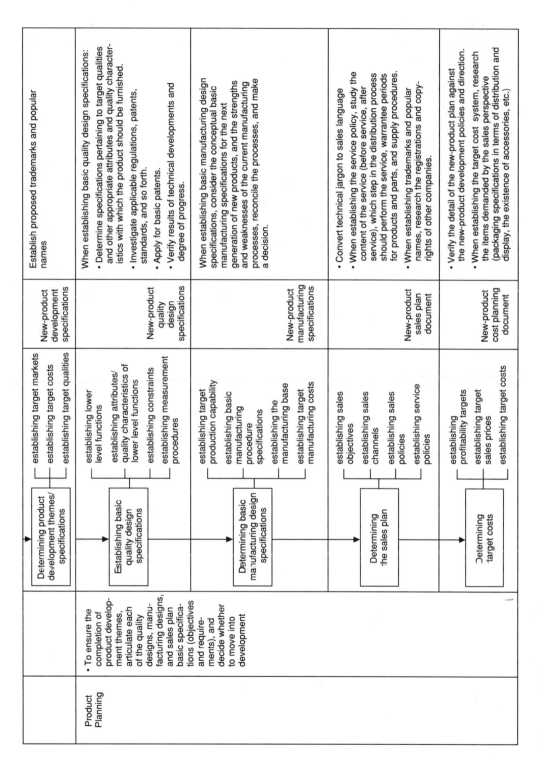

**Figure 9-2. Systematic Diagram of Product Planning**

4. Establish a product planning system, clearly define the tasks and control procedures for each step, standardize the system, and then improve the product planning procedures and system.

5. Define the hoshin of products that should be developed.

6. Perform patent management (fill out patent applications, research rights of other companies).

7. Ensure continuity in the product planning process by verifying the purposes of each step, checking the agreement between objectives and actual results at the completion of each step, and determining for each step whether a transfer can be made to the next step in the process.

8. Standardize the technical details and management methods gained through a new-product planning activity, so that new-product planning in the next period becomes easier to execute.

9. When a step in the established product plan is skipped, clearly define the reason for skipping it.

10. Define in advance the necessary data, control methods, and materials, and control progress.


## EXAMPLES OF PROBLEM-SOLVING ACTIVITIES IN THE PRODUCT PLANNING DEPARTMENT[1]

The Electric Shaver Division of Matsushita Electric Works, Ltd. is involved in developing, producing, and marketing electric shavers. Since it began production in 1955, it has untiringly pursued basic technologies in its quest to provide "the finest shaves in the world." Despite selling to a highly mature market, the company is able to stimulate new demand and maintain the top domestic market share in Japan.

Developing new products that receive high user evaluations contributes greatly to fiscal results. Because of this, thorough market surveys and product planning that is directly connected to the users are important. In the Electric Shaver Division, emphasis was placed on defining those processes of product

---

[1] Shigeru Mizuno and Yoji Akao, *Quality Function Deployment: An Approach to Total Quality Control* (Tokyo: JUSE Press, 1978).

conceptualization and product planning which had previously come to be called the "black box." Emphasis was also placed on the methods by which to incorporate the requirements for each step of product conceptualization and planning.

Below we discuss the Wet Shaver, a popular electric shaver that can be used wet and can be operated with shaving cream. The example is used to present the product planning procedures of the Electric Shaver Division of Matsushita Electric.

## Establishing the Product Development Theme

In Japan, 38 million people use shavers. An analysis of the practices of these shaver users shows that 40 percent use electric shavers, 30 percent use safety razors, and 30 percent use both. (See Figure 9-3.) When a survey was conducted investigating why the safety razor users were still using safety razors, the results shown in Figure 9-4 were obtained. We concluded that to expand the electric shaver market it is important to produce an implement that surpasses the safety razor in both the psychological and the functional aspects, as well as in safety.

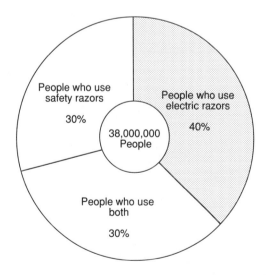

**Figure 9-3. Distribution of Shaving Population**

| Psychological Factors | • The feeling that the razor has eliminated the stubble<br>• The feeling of completeness<br>• The feeling of cleanliness |
|---|---|
| Functional Factors | • Clean shave in one pass<br>• The skin after shaving is smooth and stubble-free |
| Problem Areas | • Possibility of nicks and cuts |

**Figure 9-4. Analysis of Safety Razor Users**

Through the Wet Shaver Awareness Survey of Figure 9-5 and the Washable Shaver User Follow-Up Survey of Figure 9-6, we discovered the users' needs, and determined a concept for merchandising.

During the product conceptualization, we used the "NCP checklist" in planning. (See Figure 9-7.) This is a tool to analyze past examples of hit products and flops to determine the factors that caused the successes or failures and also to extract control points. It divides product conceptualization and product planning into three stages:

- needs (N), in which the user needs are extracted,
- concept (C), in which the product concept is established, and
- product (P), in which the product is defined.

The checklist includes items that should be checked in each of the elemental tasks. This tool increases the skills of the product planning manager and is also useful in gaining a consensus within the department about product plans.

## Establishing the Technical Development Theme

The *S-H conversion manual* is used for establishing technical issues. The S-H conversion manual takes the user needs as its starting point and converts these into technical methods when technical issues to be incorporated into the product are established. "S-H" is an abbreviation for "Soft → Hard."

Figure 9-8 shows the S-H conversion of the Wet Shaver.

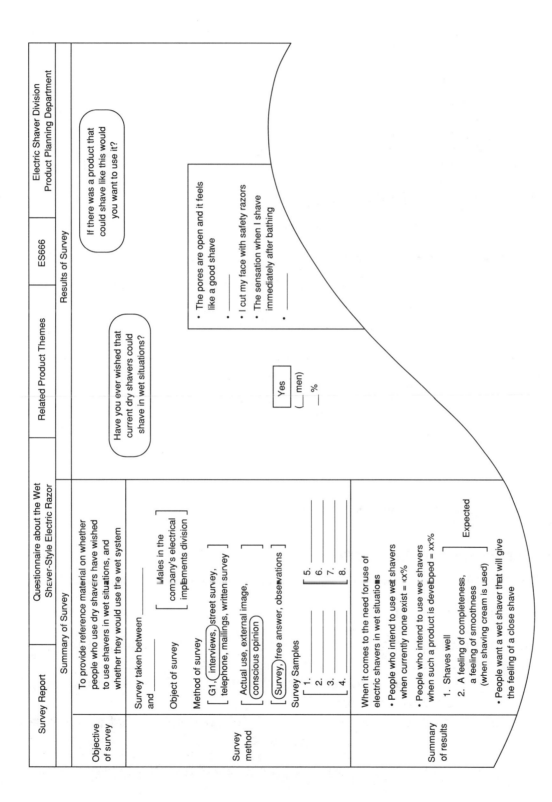

**Figure 9-5.  Wet Shaver Awareness Survey**

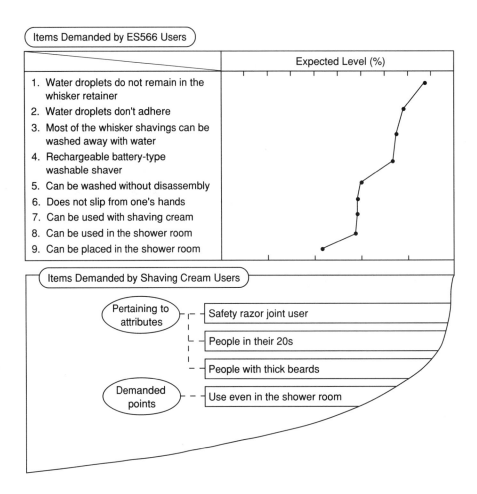

**Figure 9-6. Wet Shaver User Follow-up Survey**

## Quality Assurance in Product Planning

Quality assurance activities during product planning in Matsushita Electric's Electric Razor Division include the following:

1. Synchronizing activities at their sources in the functions and roles of each department.
2. Improving the procedures of department activities and horizontally deploying them as TQC tools.
3. Bringing management expectations into harmony so that all departments can progress through consensus.

An overview of the quality assurance concepts is presented in Figure 9-9.

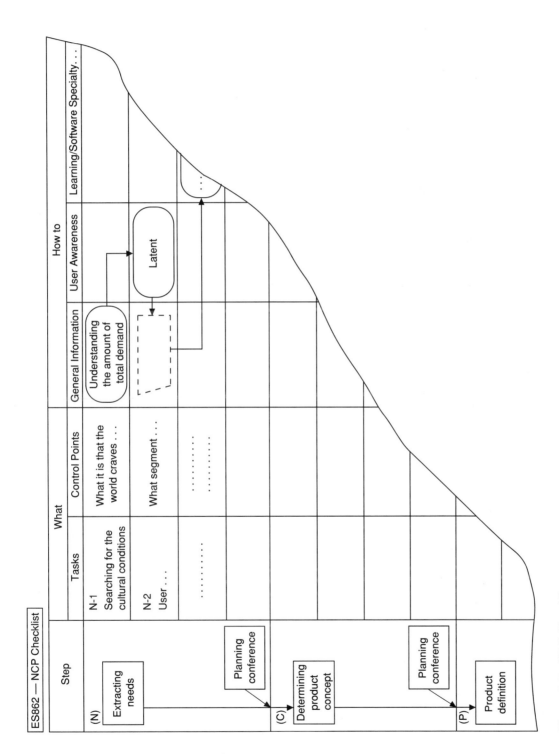

**Figure 9-7. NCP Checklist**

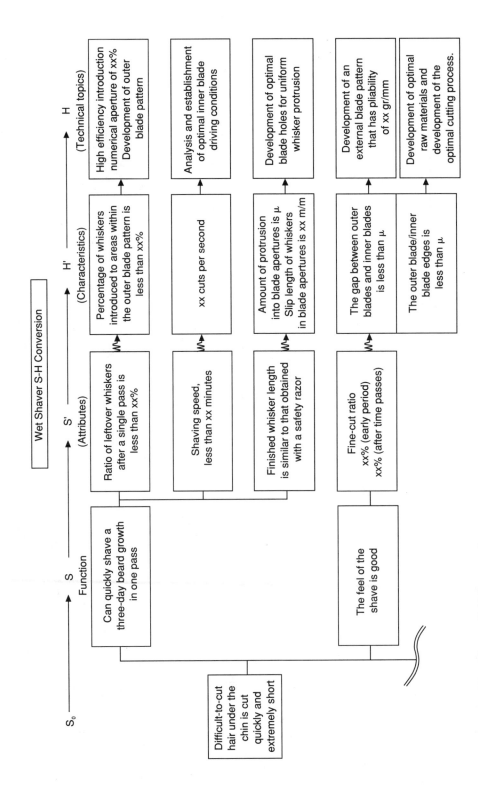

**Figure 9-8.  Wet Shaver S-H Conversion**

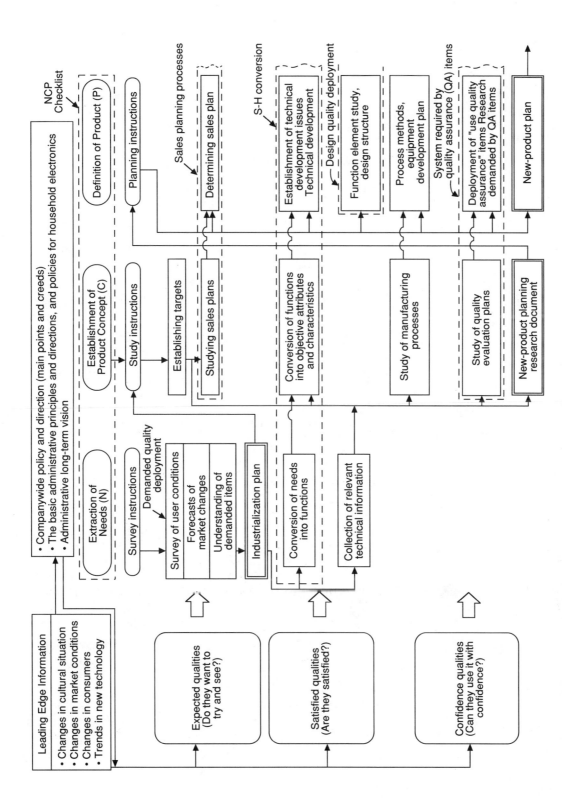

**Figure 9-9. Summary of Quality Assurance (QA) Processes in Product Planning**

# 10
# Effective Problem Solving in the Design Department

It is often said that QC is unsuited to the design department. People believe that although design depends on the abilities of the designers, and especially on individual creative innovations, the uniformity of QC systems such as standardization inhibits innovations. Can it be true that design and QC have nothing in common?

Each year customer product needs are becoming more diversified, and the environment surrounding the design department (reflecting factors such as competitive rivalry and development of products for new market-entry) is becoming even more severe, mandating that design be done in a systematic manner and with the cooperation of many departments. Because of this, systemwide objectives must be established and adhered to while the control cycle is being run.

Thus, it is not surprising that QC philosophies and methods have become necessary in the design department and that the QC approach is needed for problem solving.

## THE FUNCTION OF THE DESIGN DEPARTMENT

The design department must create the drawings and the specifications for products; ensure the qualities demanded by the users; find a balance in designs done for the manufacturing department (the "next process") between costs, production capabilities, and delivery periods; and ensure that products which satisfy the demanded qualities are produced. The following functions are considered essential to fulfillment of the design department's roles.

## Understanding the Demanded Qualities

Understanding the qualities demanded by users is crucial in new-product development and design. Hit products tend to be based not on epoch-making new technologies but on ideas that are in line with user demands. One of the requirements for corporate progress is a system of identifying demanded qualities, converting those qualities into quality characteristics, and technically developing them into products.

Although the procedures for identifying demanded qualities and the group from which these qualities should be identified vary according to industry and product, certain checkpoints are valid in each case:

- What do the users require of the product in terms of quality and cost?
- What is the product's image?
- What are the constraints in use and environment?
- How long will the product be used, and what is its durability?

In industries such as construction, where users can be readily identified, the demanded qualities can be easily sketched out. If the demanded qualities are made apparent, the design can be created while periodically checking with the users. In many cases, however, demanded qualities are in written or abstract form. Consequently, to reach a rational understanding of demanded qualities you must establish the quality characteristics and convert those characteristics into design qualities.

Figure 10-1 presents some guidelines for understanding demanded qualities in the construction industry.

## Creating and Visualizing the Design Qualities

The qualities demanded by users must be converted into design qualities and expressed in a visible form that can be manufactured into products. This includes making the following items:

1. Design drawings
2. Specifications (product, component, and material specifications)

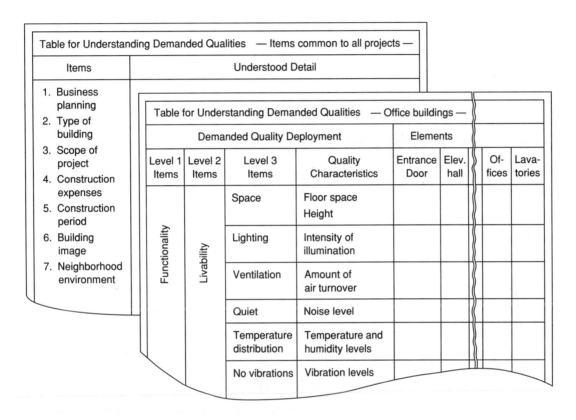

**Figure 10-1. Table for Understanding Demanded Qualities — The Construction Industry**

   3. Mock-ups or models

   4. Testing and inspection documents

If the details of the above items are incomplete, there will be complaints from the next process that: "When we manufactured it, it cost more than we had anticipated," or that "Because of the design modifications after the product reached the production stage, there have been many reworks and reprocesses, leading to problems in cost, quality, and delivery."

Although designers must rely on in-house (site) technological skills, design qualities will be improved by standardization to prevent variability due to differences between designers, by use of feedback from later processes, and by accessibility of information from within and outside the company.

The following items are topics for standardization:

• The design process manual
• Standards and manuals for making the drawings
• Materials and parts standards

Despite the obvious need to observe standards, an important part of standardization is understanding that standards are not immovable, and should be continually revised.

The following information is necessary for design:

- Standards and specifications
- Information on complaints and problems in the market and in the next process
- Samples and catalogs
- Technical materials and reports from both within and without the company
- Previous designs, specifications, and so forth
- Cost data

This information must be collected, stored, and controlled so that the designer can readily obtain it when necessary.

## Performing the Design Review

Design can be divided into three stages: planning design, basic design, and working design. Most of a product's qualities are determined during the design stage. The design review objectively evaluates the designs in each stage of the design process, proposes improvements, and verifies that the product design can pass to the next step.

However, we have often observed a tendency for people to pay too much attention to how often they get design reviews, for the timing of the reviews to be wrong, and for the reviews to only look at the fine detail instead of the big picture. To be effective, design reviews must be complete and must be run correctly.

We recommend that the following items be considered in organizing design reviews:

1. That a design review team be organized with designated experts from every field.
2. That there be an appropriate period for design reviews, and an established schedule.
3. That design reviews be run after adequate advance preparation.
4. That there be definite follow-up after the completion of design reviews.

When determining the content of the design reviews, consider the following points:

1. Make a checklist for the design review appropriate to the product being reviewed and the review items. (See Figure 10-2.)
2. Use information from the processes before and after the reviews.
3. Make definite proposals for improvement of problem areas.

| Design Review Checklist | Adjudicator | | | | |
|---|---|---|---|---|---|
| | Date | Day___Month___Year___ | | Product Name | |
| | Location | | | Code | |
| Design Review Check Items | | | | Results | Items to Note |
| 1. Appearance | | | | | |
|    a. Does the appearance satisfy the planned specifications? | | | | Pass / Fail | |
|    b. Do the dimension satisfy the planned specifications? | | | | Pass / Fail | |
| 2. Performance | | | | | |
|    a. Are the established values of characteristics appropriate? | | | | Pass / Fail | |
|    b. Is the variability in performance when mistreated within acceptable limits? | | | | Pass / Fail | |
|    c. Does it have good operability? | | | | Pass / Fail | |
| 3. Safety | | | | | |
|    a. Is it firesafe? | | | | Pass / Fail | |
|    b. Is it safe when misoperated or misused? | | | | Pass / Fail | |
|    c. Is it safe when subjected to vibrations and shocks? | | | | Pass / Fail | |
|    d. Is it safe when there are short circuits? | | | | Pass / Fail | |
| 4 Reliability | | | | | |
|    a. Have the stresses on all of the structural components been analyzed? | | | | Pass / Fail | |
|    b. Are these stresses safe? | | | | Pass / Fail | |
|    c. Was the method used to forecast expected life cycle appropriate? | | | | Pass / Fail | |

**Figure 10-2. Example of a Design Review Checklist**

Although it takes extreme diligence to prepare for, execute, and follow up after a design review, when one considers the decreased problems in the next process, the improvements in quality, and the decreases in costs, it is clear that design reviews in the future must be even more complete.

## Raising the Efficiency of the Designs

Because design problems are the most commonly experienced problems during a product's life cycle, quality designs should be emphasized. But because there are also demands for improved productivity in design departments (increases in the amount of sales per designer), it is also desirable for the designs to have greater reliability and efficiency.

Management is necessary to make and execute schedules for each step of the design process from beginning to end, as are design standardization and automation through the introduction of CAD/CAM and other systems.

To make a schedule in advance, you must be fully aware of the actual labor involved in each step of the design process. One way to do this is to examine the designers' data on the time spent in each design operation and in making the drawings for each type of product.

Another thing to consider in establishing a schedule is that the earlier in the total process a design step is found, the more time should be allocated to that step. This is because the more time that is spent on the upstream steps, the less time will have to be spent later on reworks and redesigns.

Recently, many companies have been subcontracting detail designs and equipment designs to other companies in the name of "efficiency." However, because the production department bases its production upon these drawings, subcontract quality also must be maintained.

## PROBLEM AREAS IN THE DESIGN DEPARTMENT, AND WAYS TO RESOLVE THEM

The problems that correspond to the functions of the design department, and hints for their resolution, are shown in Table 10-1. Methods to facilitate the resolution of these problem areas are included.

**Table 10-1.  Problem Areas in Design Departments, and Ways to Resolve Them**

| Functions | Problem Areas | Hints for Resolution | Methods |
|---|---|---|---|
| Understanding demanded qualities | Misunderstanding of demanded qualities. | • To understand the qualities demanded by many unspecified users, companies often use questionnaires and surveys analyzing their results with multivariate analysis.<br>• When the users can be specifically determined, the designers can ask the users directly what the demanded qualities are.<br>• Whatever the case, it is important that the system by which the demanded qualities of the relevant parties are understood employs the designer's knowledge and adequately considers consumer's needs. | Multivariate analysis<br><br>Quality Function Deployment |
| | Conversion of demanded qualities into quality characteristics is done poorly | • For each of the elements, make tools to convert from functions to quality characteristics, and thus reduce the variability among designers.<br>• Use multivariate analysis to convert demanded qualities, stated in terms of sensory expressions, to quality characteristics. | Quality function deployment<br><br>Multivariate analysis |
| Incorporating design qualities | Information about problems on the manufacturing floor is not used in the designs. | • Although action is taken in response to each complaint pointed out by the next process, many of the corrective actions are merely first-aid measures, there being no systematic accumulation and use of information, such as complaints and suggestions for improvements, which have been fed back to the previous process.<br>• Feedback is inadequate because the responsibilities and tasks of feedback collection are not adequately defined, or because the data that should be collected are not specified.<br>• Also, even if data are collected, they must be analyzed and processed so that designers can use them.<br>• Consequently, the responsibilities and tasks of collecting, analyzing, and processing data must be clearly defined. | Relations diagrams<br><br>Cause-and-effect diagrams<br><br>Pareto charts<br><br>Design of experiments methods<br><br>Checklists<br><br>Quality function deployment |

| Category | Symptom | Recommendation | Tools |
|---|---|---|---|
| | Costs are inadequately understood. | • If cost overruns become apparent in the later design processes, it causes a great deal of redesign and lost time. Therefore, it is extremely important to accurately understand costs in the early stages of the design process.<br>• Often the roots to problems in understanding costs are that the cost data being used doesn't reflect reality and the forecasting methods are inaccurate. These points should be improved. | Relations diagrams<br>Cause-and-effect diagrams<br>Scatter diagrams<br>Simple regression analysis<br>Multiple regression analysis |
| | There are too many design reworks. | • Perform a design process analysis to determine what, specifically, is being reworked and redesigned too often. | Pareto charts |
| | The design reviews are not being performed at the appropriate times. | • For design reviews to be effective, they must be performed at the appropriate time. A schedule must be determined at the beginning of the design process, and the organization of the design review team must be clearly defined. | Arrow diagrams<br>New-product development system diagrams |
| Executing design reviews | The contents of the design reviews are too formalized and lack meaning | • If the advance preparation of the design review team is inadequate, then the design reviews will not be effective. Consequently, the design review teams must take adequate time in advance for preparations.<br>• With checklists using information such as examples of failures from the past, the design reviews can be made highly effective.<br>• It is necessary to faithfully follow up on designated items. | Checklists |
| Raising the efficiency of design | There is variability in the labor content of designs. | • Make a formula through which the labor content of designs can be calculated from past data.<br>• To do this, collect data from the designers about each task which they perform.<br>• The earlier the design step is found in the design process, the more weight must be placed on the forecasts for the labor content of that step. Set targets, and control the processes accordingly. | Simple regression analysis<br>Multiple regression analysis<br>Operations analysis |
| | The efficiency of the design process cannot be improved sufficiently through control of design labor content. | • Controlling design labor content is a procedure wherein target design labor content levels are set and then compared with actual results. Actual increases in efficiency require improvement activities such as automation and standardization. | Checklists |

# 11
# Effective Problem Solving in the Production Engineering Department

Japan's production engineering is considered to be the best in the world. That many Japanese products today are eclipsing European and American products is a result of the cumulative efforts of production engineering departments to "make good products economically."

The production engineering department performs many activities to create an efficient manufacturing system and to reconcile manufacturing qualities with design qualities in accordance with the manufacturing product plan, which was designed and established by the development department (through research and development, design, testing, trials, and so forth). While using mechanical engineering, electrical engineering, chemical engineering, and all types of site-specific technologies to perform this work, you should establish a management system through a managerial engineering approach incorporating QC attitudes and philosophies. In this section we discuss the work of production engineering, focusing on this managerial engineering concept.

In managing production engineering you determine what is important according to industry and product, according to whether you are dealing with a market-production or a customer-order situation, and according to whether the production is done job shop-style or mass production-style. In this section we discuss general problem solving in production engineering.

## THE FUNCTION OF THE PRODUCTION ENGINEERING DEPARTMENT

The major functions of the production engineering department are as follows:

1. Development and introduction of new production technologies (new materials, new processing technologies, etc.)
2. Preparation for new-product production (process planning, equipment planning, equipping processes, etc.)
3. Assertive approaches to planning labor economization (equipment investment plan)
4. Provision of production engineering information to the planning/ design departments

### Development and Introduction of New Production Technologies

The development of production technologies is a multifaceted task, including the development of materials, process technologies, electronics, measurement technology, and systems. And even if you took just one of these elements, say, the development of materials, you must still consider (1) development aimed at current technologies, such as improving yields, reducing processes, and replacing materials, and (2) development of absolutely new materials aimed at improving the amount of value added. These types of development must synchronize with the development of new products. Consequently, the company's policy must be clear about which technologies the company should develop itself and which should be brought in from elsewhere. For the technologies to be developed in-house, decisions must be made about the budgets and schedules (using arrow diagrams) for the development of the technology. A qualified and committed engineer must be chosen to lead the project and the development must be tracked.

### Making Preparations for the Production of New Products

The task in this step is to prepare, before production commences, the four elements of production: machines and equipment, raw materials and parts, manufacturing and measurement methods, and employees. You must also prepare the necessary tools, measuring implements, and so forth. This step is especially important in the case of new products, because the quality of the preparation determines the success or failure of the early production. While the production engineering department is clearly defining problem areas with the existing products or processes, it should also be executing the control cycle and including in the preparations for production corrective action plans to completely cure those problems:

- Including corrective actions to quality problems (if there are problems found in the marketplace, these problems are treated as top priority)
- Maintaining and improving process capabilities
- Modifying equipment and introducing newly produced equipment (while reexamining the distinctions between equipment produced in-house and that purchased)
- Including in the preparations VE and energy conservation measures

Below we show the standard procedures followed in this stage:

1. Establishing and adjusting the master schedule for the beginning of manufacturing
2. Making make-or-buy decisions on portions of the process and directing the vendor's production preparations
3. Making process plans in accordance with design qualities
4. Making the equipment plan and procuring the equipment
5. Equipping the processes (verifying process capability, equipping and improving standards, etc.)
6. Securing necessary personnel, education, and training
7. Executing a verification trial before production begins
   - executing a final verification trial of established equipment, processes, and parts
   - verifying the conformance of the standards

## Managing the Equipment Investment Plan

An important task of the production engineering department is to oversee a new equipment investment plan to reduce labor costs and rationalize the processes. Although the department must also promote activities to reduce labor content, mostly by reducing waste, it must at the same time introduce equipment with new technology on a timely basis, watching trends in the economy and in demand, and also remaining aware of the company's management position.

After clearly defining the company's technological and economic needs, the production engineering department must submit proposals for necessary equipment investments to the accounting department and the administrative planning departments. Equipment investment evaluation criteria relating to the labor reduction plan should be established at this time. Moreover, equipment for rationalizing processes can most realistically be introduced during the preparations for the manufacture of new products.

## Providing Production Engineering Information to the Planning and Design Department

If the planning and design departments are so idealistic they demand design qualities (standards, drawings, and the like) that ignore the factory process capability, and if on the other hand the manufacturing floor cannot accommodate these standards and instructions but instead is left crying over a mountain of reworks, then the company gains nothing.

Along with providing, in a timely manner, information about process capabilities to the upstream planning and design steps, the production engineering department should anticipate changes in the demanded qualities of the market, and study well in advance strategies to adapt to those changes. It is important to establish a system to achieve this. It is also important that trends in production engineering be included in the new-product development process through cooperation between the production engineering and the planning and design departments.

## PROBLEM AREAS IN THE PRODUCTION ENGINEERING DEPARTMENT, AND WAYS TO RESOLVE THEM

The problems that correspond to the functions of the production engineering department, and hints for their resolution, are shown in Table 11-1 (see pages 62-63). QC philosophies and methods to facilitate the resolution of these problem areas are also included.

## AN EXAMPLE OF PROBLEM SOLVING IN THE PRODUCTION ENGINEERING DEPARTMENT

In this section we describe the preparations for production of a new casting part. We hope that this example will serve as a reference for investigating processes and improving equipment and processes. The theme of the improvement activities is "Preparations for production of new products involving reduced-weight cast parts."

### Process Planning

1. *Quality characteristics:* This new product will reduce the weight of the existing product by 10 percent. It will fulfill the necessary functions yet contain no wasted filling.
2. *Product shapes and processes:* See Figure 11-1.
3. *Process investigation:* See Figure 11-2.
4. *Investigation of causes of variability in wall thicknesses:* See Figures 11-3 through 11-5.
5. *Corrective action:*
   - Reducing the impacts on the metal frames during transport → *equipment planning*
   - Reducing core deformations → *individual process improvement*

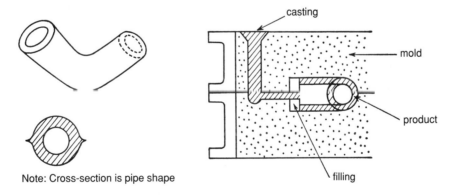

Note: Cross-section is pipe shape

**Figure 11-1. Shape of Product and Casting Method**

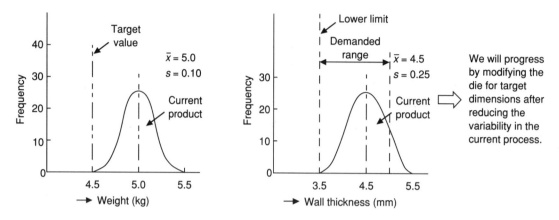

**Figure 11-2. Weight of Current Product and Target Weight; Wall Thickness and Demanded Range**

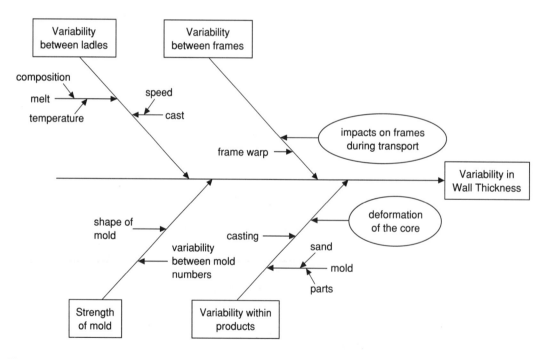

**Figure 11-3. Cause-and-effect Diagram of Variability in Wall Thickness**

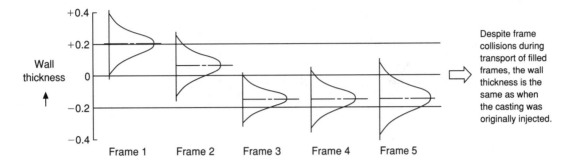

Despite frame collisions during transport of filled frames, the wall thickness is the same as when the casting was originally injected.

**Figure 11-4. Changes in Wall Thickness According to Frames**

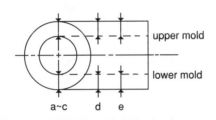

Description of locations (a - e)

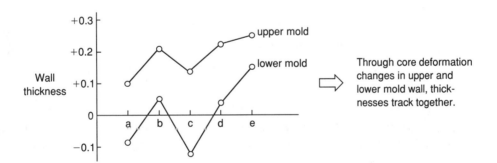

Through core deformation changes in upper and lower mold wall, thicknesses track together.

**Figure 11-5. Explanation of Locations (a - e) and Differences of Wall Thickness within Product**

## Equipment Planning

1. *Objective:*
   • To improve the metal frame transport process
   • To improve the shock-absorbent fixtures
2. *Equipment improvement:* See Figure 11-6.

## Individual Process Improvement

1. *Corrective action for core deformations during injection:* See Figure 11-7.
2. *Maintaining shell wall thickness:* We investigated the effects of core firing temperature and firing time on the wall thickness. (See Table 11-2.) We found that the longer the firing time, the better the shell wall thickness was maintained. (See Table 11-3.)
3. *Study of core sand brands:* Having tested various types of sand, we changed the grain of sand we were using in the core (to a finer grain).

## Integrated Process Improvement

1. *Corrective action for sand inclusion defects:* Because sand inclusion defects (5 cores out of 62) resulted from our changing the parameters of the core fabrication process, we implemented a corrective action. (See Figure 11-8.)
2. *Maintaining core mold dimensions (by increasing firing time):* To secure the firing time, we
   • increased the number of molds used
   • improved the shell blow process method
3. *Modifying the mold target values:* We used statistical methods to determine a mold adjustment value and performed test castings for verifications.
4. *Verifying the state of process improvement:* See Figures 11-9 and 11-10.

## Results

See Figure 11-11.

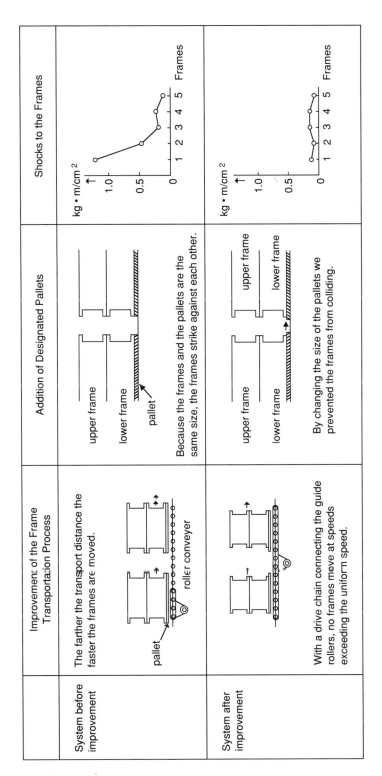

**Figure 11-6. Improvement of Equipment to Absorb Shocks to the Frames**

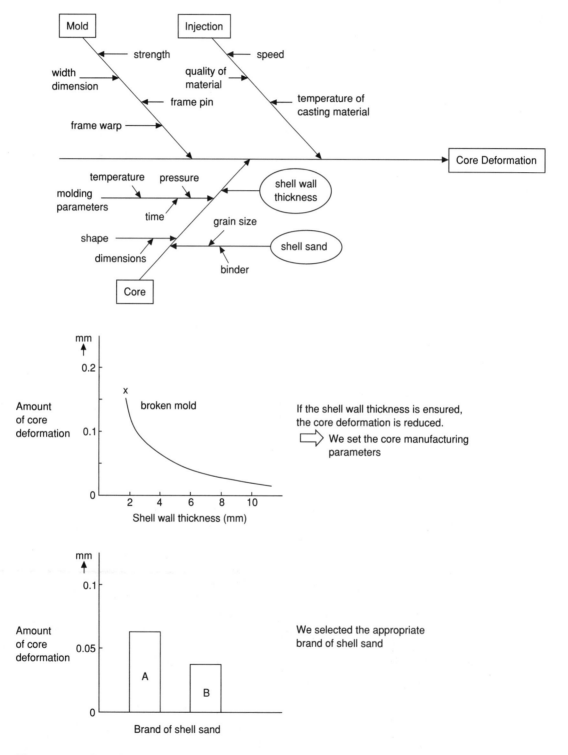

**Figure 11-7.  Core Deformation Corrective Action**

**Table 11-2. Shell Thickness Data (mm)**

| | | Firing Time (sec) | | |
|---|---|---|---|---|
| | | 20 | 40 | 60 |
| Core firing temperature (°C) | 340 | 5.0 | 9.5 | 12.0 |
| | 300 | 4.5 | 6.0 | 9.5 |
| | 260 | 4.0 | 5.5 | 8.0 |

**Table 11-3. Analysis of Variance Table**

| Factor | Sum of Squares | Degrees of Freedom | Mean Square | Variance Ratio |
|---|---|---|---|---|
| Core firing temperature | 57.6 | 2 | 28.8 | 8.0 |
| Firing time | 171.6 | 2 | 85.8 | 23.8* |
| Residual | 14.4 | 4 | 3.6 | |
| Total | 243.6 | 8 | | |

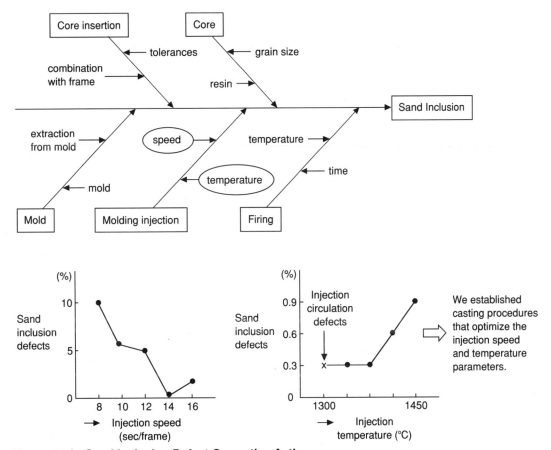

**Figure 11-8. Sand Inclusion Defect Corrective Action**

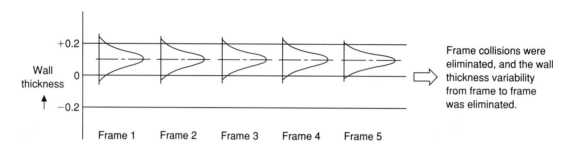

**Figure 11-9.  Differences in Wall Thicknesses between Frames (After Equipment Improvements)**

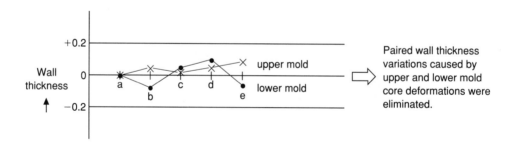

**Figure 11-10.  Product Wall Thickness (Core Deformation)**

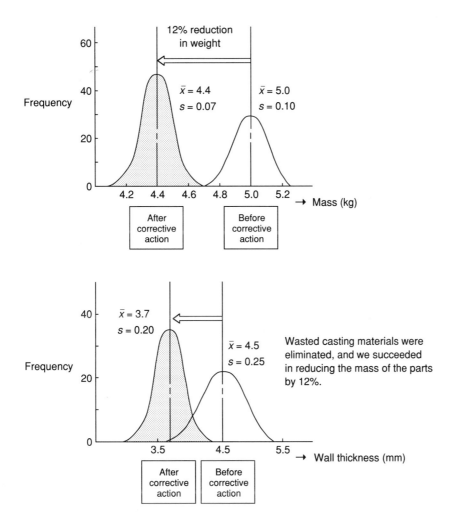

**Figure 11-11. Weight Reduction Effects and Wall-thinning Effects After Corrective Action**

**Table 11-1. Problem Areas in Production Engineering Department, and Ways to Resolve Them**

| Functions | Problem Areas | Hints for Resolution | QC Philosophies and Methods |
|---|---|---|---|
| 1. Development and introduction of new production techniques (new materials, new processing techniques, electronics, etc.) | (1) The timing of the development of new production techniques is not favorable, or in harmony with new-product development. | • Define new materials and new processing techniques that should be included in the development of the next generation of new products; shortening the time it takes to make developments; and coordinate the timing of developments with new-product developments.<br>• Educate engineers to pioneer new developments. | Arrow diagrams<br>Developing personal creative powers (creativity engineering) |
| | (2) The development of new production techniques is being neglected because all the time is spent in activities such as preparing for the manufacture of new products and improving equipment capacities in preparation for increased production. | • Make estimations of standard production preparation labor content based on the pattern of the labor used in the past for projects of the same size. Adjust time allocation decisions according to the needs of sales and according to the date set for the beginning of sales of other projects. | Control of labor content, emphasis on priorities |
| 2. Preparation for manufacturing new products | (1) To meet the needs of the consumers in this time of diversification of needs and severe market competition, we have shortened our time for development and now don't have enough time to bring up production. | • Reconcile schedules, including the target dates when Sales says that it must release the product, the feasible dates that the design drawings can be ready, and the responsibilities shouldered by every department that must make preparations for the manufacturing (including the departments that must lay in inventory).<br>• Study ways to shorten the lead times of the especially critical items, and track and control the progress of these critical items while working for an overall contraction of schedules. | Consumer orientation<br>Arrow diagrams |
| | (2) Internal sourcing versus external sourcing decisions must be made based on management policy and on the long-term plan and must include adequate research into costs. | • Make overall decision for internal sourcing versus external sourcing, using cost comparisons including management policies, long-term equipment investment plans, the load on the existing equipment, items related to strategies for purchasing from vendors, transportation costs, and so forth.<br>• Use specialty manufacturers outside of the company.<br>  1. High levels of specialized knowledge about electronic components, etc.<br>  2. Use of standard market components. | Standardization (making company policies)<br>Engineering economy<br>Methods<br>Information management |
| | (3) Because process plans are not made based on understanding process capabilities, there are processes that have a hard time ensuring design qualities. | • Research what types of processes are necessary to build the design qualities into the products and then establish the manufacturing methods.<br>• Establish equipment capabilities and lay out design.<br>• Estimating total equipment investment and labor content and materials costs/unit.<br>• When necessary, enlist the participation of the manufacturing department, listening to their opinions and desires. | Process capability studies<br>IE (including time studies)<br>Equipment investment profitability calculations |

| | | |
|---|---|---|
| (4) The concepts of energy conservation, PM, and VE are not adequately worked into the equipment plans. Also, equipment is received without first having adequate safety checks and verifications of precision. | • Research necessary equipment, including energy conservation issues, PM and VE issues. Circulate a design for feedback.<br>• Research vendors.<br>• Devise and reconcile equipment procurement schedules and layout and construction plans.<br>• Perform safety checks, and verify equipment operations, functions, and precision (including dies and jigs) through a standing committee. | Energy conservation<br>PM<br>VE<br>Bar charts and arrow diagrams<br>The "safety first" concept |
| (5) Because the corrective actions for problems and the process improvements made through the results of the trial use of the newly introduced equipment are inadequate, many problems occur after production begins. | • Use the newly introduced equipment in a line trial run.<br>1. Verify process capabilities, production capacity, and manufacturability.<br>2. Expose and improve problems with quality or operability.<br>• Verify harmony with standards (quality standards, operational standards, QC process charts, operations summary documents, etc.)<br>• Establish standard times. | Stratification and analysis<br>Quality assurance system |
| 3. Addressing of labor economization plans | | |
| (1) Poor timing with equipment investment for labor economization and rationalization causes the company to lose the ability to compete within the industry, threatening the continued existence of company. | • Fully establish a long-term equipment investment plan based upon the management policies and direction, and upon the strength of the company.<br>• Clearly define the criteria for equipment investment for rationalization (e.g., the acceptable equipment investment per worker displaced).<br>• Assertively work rationalization equipment investments into the equipment plans, which go along with the preparations to manufacture new products.<br>• Understand the trends in the development of new production techniques, and if necessary establish within the company a development system (e.g., the introduction of robots). | Establishment of management plans<br>Coefficients of investment recovery (the MAPI theory)<br>New-product cost plans |
| (2) The labor-saving equipment improvements to prepare for the aging of the work force are going slowly. | • To prepare for the future, systematically improve the equipment in processes where the working conditions are bad, where mass-produced products are made by hand, etc. | IE |
| 4. Provision of data on production techniques to the planning and the design departments. | | |
| (1) There is poor cooperation with the planning and design departments, and they are slow to utilize new production techniques. Also, they demand design qualities that ignore the manufacturing process capabilities. | • Communicate new developments in the production techniques to upstream planning and design departments in a timely manner, and work these developments into design modifications and new-product developments. (For example, new developments in production techniques that incorporate manufacturing parameters not allowed by the old processes can greatly reduce costs.)<br>• Provide upstream departments with current processes capability data. | Control at the Source<br>Process capability studies |

# 12

# Effective Problem Solving in the Manufacturing Department

In manufacturing industries, products with stable quality can be produced only after the manufacturing floor is brought to a controlled state. QC began as an attempt to apply statistical theory to the field of manufacturing; indeed, the introduction of QC to a company usually begins on the manufacturing floor. Fortunately, a great many data can be collected from the results of production activities, and circumstances on manufacturing floors are such that there is great freedom in selecting problem areas and themes for improvement. In addition, in manufacturing companies the department with the most employees is usually the manufacturing department. A QC program based in this area producing excellent results will increase the strength of the company as a whole. Therefore, it is important to optimize the effectiveness of the manufacturing floor.

## CONTROL OF PROCESSES (CONTROL THAT MAINTAINS THE STATUS QUO)

The fundamental mission of a manufacturing floor is to maintain processes in a stable state to produce products with qualities that are in agreement with the quality targets. It is thus important to establish procedures for process control and then to follow the set procedures exactly. Once this is done, you should study the corrective actions necessary to handle aberrant conditions or problems when they are discovered — even if it means temporarily stopping the line.

## Establishing the Form of Process Control

It is usual to compile the process control procedures into a QC process chart. The items in this chart include the following:

1. Control items
2. Control characteristics
3. Control levels/control ranges
4. Methods of control charting (who draws in the control limits and plots points, and when)
5. The method of judging the status of control (recognizing out-of-control conditions)
6. Procedures for handling out-of-control conditions (how to trace the causes of problems, who should do it, and who reports what to whom, for example)

An example of a form for QC process charts is given in Figure 12-1.

| QC Process Chart    Department _____  Construction Name _____ | | | | | | | | | | Date Compiled | Approval Stamp | Created By |
|---|---|---|---|---|---|---|---|---|---|---|---|---|
| | | | | | | | | | | Creation | | |
| | | | | | | | | | | Revision | | |
| | | | | | | | | | | Revision | | |
| Process | | Control Items | Control Level | Control Methods | | | | Problem Management | | Responsible Manager | Related Standards Documents | Notes |
| Chart | Unit Process | Control Items | Control Level | Fre-quency | Measure-ment Method | Control Materials | Respon-sible Party | Method | Responsible Party | Responsible Manager | Related Standards Documents | Notes |
| | | | | | | | | | | | | |

**Figure 12-1. Example of a QC Process Chart**

Also, the correct operational procedures are defined in the operational standards. The writers and the users of these documents must work together innovatively to develop documents that are easily used.

## Performing the Standardized Operations

Each worker should adopt the attitudes that "Each individual is the champion of the work" and "The next process is the customer." Each worker should also accept responsibility for the work he or she has done as an individual. Thus, each person must understand what is included in the operational specifications, and execute it with precision. (See Figure 12-2.)

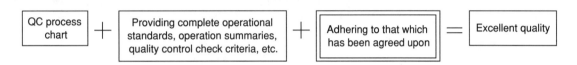

**Figure 12-2. Thorough Standardized Operations**

However, because "following established procedures" seems simple to do, it is frequently not thoroughly done. To raise the level of quality consciousness on the work floor, you must educate and train operators.

Above all, you must thoroughly practice the 5-S's of *Seiri* (organizing), *Seiton* (arranging), *Seiketsu* (cleanliness), *Seiso* (cleaning), and *Shitsuke* (discipline).

## Handling Process Problems and Preventing Recurrence

The existence of process aberrations should be determined by use of control charts upon which there are rationally determined control limits. When you detect problems in this way, you can assume that something in the process has changed. You should then search for the root cause of this change and take corrective action to eradicate the cause and prevent it from recurring. (See Figure 12-3.)

In the case of the most important processes, such as those for safety equipment, you need to establish a system that prevents recurrence by ensuring that incorrect operations cannot be performed. *Poka-yoke* (mistake-proofing) systems are one type of recurrence-prevention system. An example of poka-yoke is given in Figure 12-4.

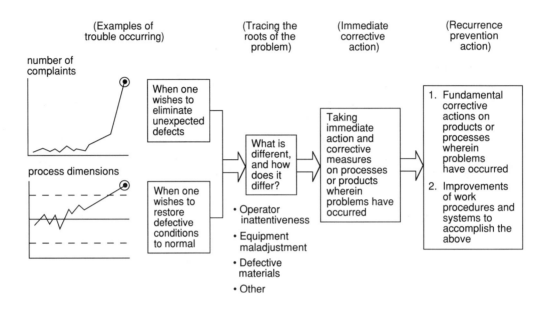

**Figure 12-3. Corrective Action to Handle Problems and Prevent Recurrences**

| Objective of the Poka-yoke Devices | Important Points in the Devices | Sketch of Device |
|---|---|---|
| Example 1: Preventing work from being transferred to the next station if welds have been forgotten | When the correct number of spot welds have been performed, a counter-relay sends a signal to the chute, which opens the shutter and sends the work to the next station. (A photocell senses when the work has been sent to the next station and closes the shutter.) | |
| Example 2: Preventing the next machining process when a casting fin is remaining in the injection hole | The machining process equipment is outfitted with a poka-yoke pin, so the part is raised if there is a casting fin and cannot be placed on the jig. | |

**Figure 12-4. Example of a Poka-yoke System**

## Deployment of Integrated Control

Because processes are controlled in terms of the results of the work — which include all aspects of quality, cost, delivery, and safety — the "control items" include not just the quality of the product, but also cost, safety, and so forth. "Control" should be deployed in terms of integrated control. For example, the following items should be addressed and supported:

- *Quality:* Number of complaints, direct processing rates (ratio of products that complete the manufacturing process without need of special handling or reworks), process defect rates, and so on.
- *Cost:* Productivity (per machine, per worker, per day, etc.), labor content per unit, basic units of materials, recovery rates (yields), energy expenses, scrap expenses, and so on.
- *Delivery:* State of progress as related to the daily plan, on-time delivery rates, and so on.
- *Safety:* Number of accidents, number of continuous days without an accident, frequency ratios, strength ratios, and so on.

## IMPROVEMENT OF PROCESSES (CONTROL THAT DISRUPTS THE STATUS QUO)

Although stability of processes is important, by itself it is not sufficient. You must also make improvements, while still precisely following the standards. Improvement activities (kaizen) include both improvement to the next level of quality, cost, delivery, or safety, and improvement (reduction) of variability. (See Figure 12-5.)

Also, although the process of determining an improvement problem is covered in detail in Chapter 3, carefully consider the following items while making decisions.

1. Make decisions in light of the plans (such as the long-term company plan or the yearly company plan), policies, and directions from above.
2. Emphasize those areas suggested as needing improvement in the past.
3. Address problems that respond to changing market conditions or changes in equipment or materials.

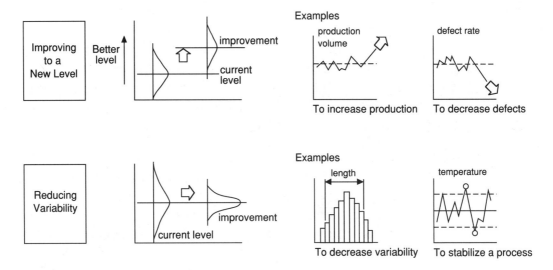

**Figure 12-5. Finding Problems That Require Process Improvements**

Next we discuss specific steps in process improvement. Certainly, the steps of the problem-solving process described in Chapter 4 should be followed closely. Here, however, we discuss the method of problem solving in the manufacturing department, emphasizing *the role of middle management.*

1. Middle managers should visit the manufacturing floor as often as possible, verifying actual circumstances by personally checking on them. They should thoroughly base their management activities on facts.
2. Process control should be constantly monitored through use of graphs and control charts; problem areas and questionable areas should be noted.
3. Along with having a broad scope of vision, middle managers should be looking into the future when forming key themes for their work areas, and should provide direction for workers.
4. To do this, middle managers should visit other companies to get ideas, and consider how to apply these ideas to their own work areas.

Middle managers should exhibit leadership and be on the forefront of process control and improvement. Below we discuss the roles and actions of middle managers from the perspectives of policy hoshin deployment and QC circles.

## Policy Deployment

Middle managers should examine the important problems within their own departments that require a change in status quo, relate these to company policies, and from these establish their own policies. These policies should be defined in an execution plan, and the execution activities must be tracked and their results verified. Figure 12-6 is an example of policy deployment in regard to body roof leaks.

## Fostering QC Circles

Out of respect for the individual, and to create a workplace that is conducive to work and to the valuing of work, middle managers implement and cultivate QC circles. It is up to the section managers and supervisors to see that circle members willingly accept the circles as pleasant, fun activities. Education to ensure an understanding of QC circle activities and to motivate workers, and education and training in QC problem solving are especially important during implementation of QC circle activities. Once the activities have produced results, then continuing development can be ensured through regular meetings in which the results of the activities are presented.

According to a survey, the greatest impediments to the progress of QC circles (*Quality Control for the Foreman*, No. 209) are the following:

1. Lack of ability or leadership in the circle leader
2. Normal job requirements that are too demanding, leaving no time for circle activities
3. Difficulty in selecting and analyzing themes
4. Circle members who don't know each other well enough and so are afraid to speak out in the meetings and don't cooperate well

It is the responsibility of the section managers and supervisors to work with circle leaders and members to overcome these problems.

The following items serve as criteria for evaluating the level of activity of QC Circles:

- The number of themes resolved by each circle in a year's time — 4 or more.

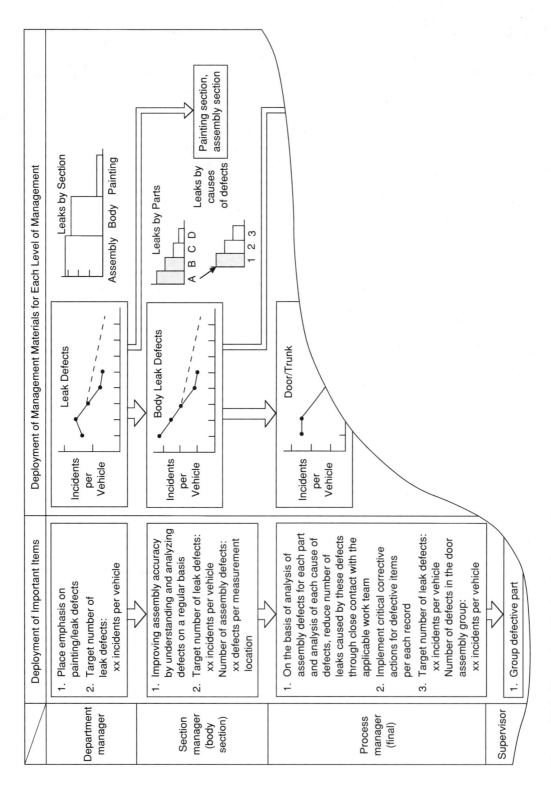

**Figure 12-6.   Example of Policy Deployment**

- The number of suggestions for improvement in one year's time — 12 or more per person.
- Money saved through the results — ¥200,000 per circle member per year (about $1,400 at an exchange rate of ¥143 per $1).
- Number of circle meetings — 24 or more per year.
- Circle meeting time — 2 or more hours per month
- Attendance rates of members — 91 percent or more.

Furthermore, middle managers must recognize that QC circle activities supplement normal work activities. Of all of the problems that are discovered, many will not be addressed by the QC circles but instead will be addressed by regular managers in the performance of their own jobs.

We have compiled the important points of process control and process improvement, the applicable QC philosophies and methods, and the application checkpoints in Table 12-1. This table can serve as a references in process control and process improvement activities.

## AN EXAMPLE OF PROBLEM SOLVING IN THE MANUFACTURING DEPARTMENT

As an example of problem solving in the manufacturing department, we offer a presentation made in the JUSE 66th QC Basic Course (Osaka) Individual Research Group, "Reducing Broken Warp Threads," by Tetsuo Uragaki of the Factory of Tōyō Bōseki.

### Summary of Process

The threads that we ship to the users function as the lengthwise threads in textile weaving. The machine that prepares the lengthwise threads is called a warper (WP), and the number of threads that break during the warping process has become a problem. (See Figure 12-7.)

### Reason for Selection of Theme

Of all of the complaints received in 1983, broken warp threads constituted the greatest portion (see Figure 12-8). We selected this theme in order to reduce the number of broken threads.

**Table 12-1. Checkpoints and Important Points in Process Control and Process Improvement**

| | | Checkpoints |
|---|---|---|
| | | **PDCA Checkpoints in Process Control** |
| Control of processes (control to maintain the status quo) | Plan (P) | 1. Do you understand the quality characteristics that make the customer happy?<br>2. Are the relationships with quality and the 4Ms (machines, method, materials, man) clearly defined?<br>3. Are there established standards documents (operational and engineering standards, etc.)?<br>4. Are the standards correctly understood?<br>5. Are there established procedures to create, revise, and control standards documents?<br>6. Do standards to include opinions of engineers, QA, and the workers?<br>7. Are easily executed operational procedures, common sense items, and cautions included in the operational standards?<br>8. Are there established procedures for handling equipment, jigs, and measuring tools?<br>9. Are there procedures for handling process aberrations and people who must be contacted?<br>10. Is there adequate education and training about the detail of the operational standards and the significance of the standard procedures? |
| | Do (D) | 1. Are the operations definitely being done according to standards?<br>2. Are materials, equipment, jigs, measuring tools, and so forth being provided according to standards?<br>3. Do operator assignments consider individuals abilities and characteristics?<br>4. Are the lighting, ventilation, and temperature appropriate? |
| | Check (C) | 1. Are the operations going as directed?<br>2. Are checks performed using QC methods such as check sheets and control charts?<br>3. Are checks performed on cause factors as well as results?<br>4. Do the floor managers perform regular rounds of the work floor? |
| | Action (A) | 1. Are the criteria for recognizing aberrations clearly defined?<br>2. When aberrations are discovered, are there specified people to inform, methods by which to inform them, and people responsible for corrective actions?<br>3. Is action quickly taken when there are process aberrations?<br>4. Is there sufficient investigation as to the causes of the aberrations?<br>5. Are recurrence prevention plans put in place?<br>6. Are proactive measures being taken?<br>7. Are poka-yoke systems being used?<br>8. Are actions on products being distinguished from actions on processes?<br>9. Do the actions have any detrimental side effects?<br>10. Are the standards revised and anti-backslide measures put in place? |
| | | **Improvement of processes (control to disrupt the status quo)** |

Note 1: The next process should also be thought of as a user, and its needs should be included.

Note 2: Has anything become a chronic problem?

| Important Points | QC Philosophies and Methods |
|---|---|
| Faithfully execute the "control cycle" to build in quality during processes. | Control cycle |
| • Establish control systems and perform standardization. | Standardization |
| • Along with defining in the QC process chart control items, control levels, and so forth, determine the methods by which control charts are used and the actions by which to handle process aberrations. | |
| • The operational procedures are shown specifically in the operational standards. The operators who will be using these standards should assertively participate in their creation. Also, critical operations/warnings, and so forth that are displayed on the factory floor should include illustrations and sections written in red so that they are easy to see and understand. | |
| • Perform education and training for operators using actual tools, equipment, and so forth to make the education and training as practical as possible. Also, do not limit the education to the operations themselves, but include overviews of process control procedures, QC philosophy, and how to read and use control charts. (When necessary, the company should prepare appropriate educational texts.) | Education and expansion |
| • When operations cannot be performed according to standards, stop the line and study corrective actions. (Defects are not passed to the next process.) | "The next process is the customer." |
| • Along with thoroughly executing the 5S's, so that unusual circumstances are readily apparent, the floor manager should regularly inspect the work floor. | Fact control |
| • Along with defining criteria by which to recognize problems, clearly define, through 5W1H, the action to be taken when problems are discovered. | Variability control |
| • Take swift, definite action in response to problems and prevent recurrence by revising engineering and operational standards accordingly. | Recurrence prevention |
| • Perform thorough stratified control of critical processes; display control materials in such a way that anyone can understand them; perform necessary operator education; and allow only qualified operators to run the processes. | Stratification |
| • Thoroughly perform alteration control. Because problems often arise when processes, equipment, operations, etc., are modified, perform special control pertaining to early products after changes. | |
| Promote control, centered on middle management, to disrupt the status quo. | |
| (1) Promoting policy management: Deploy topics, target levels, strategies, procedures, and schedules, about which the current circumstances should be changed. The results of execution should be carefully followed and verified. | Policy management |
| (2) Analysis of critical quality problems should begin with the formation of a project team. Quality problems should be addressed in order of the size of expected results. | Priority emphasis |
| (3) While raising problem consciousness, help the workers to autonomously seek problem areas and perform analysis using QC methods. Do this by introducing and fostering QC circles. Use these QC circle activities to target the creation of a workshop that is conducive to high performance and individual motivation. | QC circle activities The use of QC methods Respect for the individual |
| (4) Provide education about the steps of problem solving, the QC story, QC methods, and so forth. | The steps of problem solving The QC story |

The letters P, D, C, A appear vertically along the left side of the upper table section indicating the control cycle (Plan, Do, Check, Act).

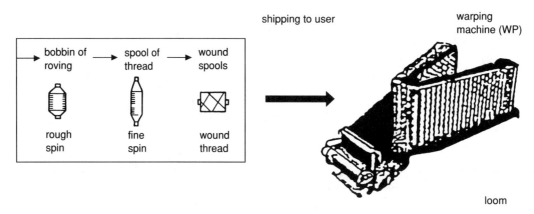

**Figure 12-7.  Diagram of Process**

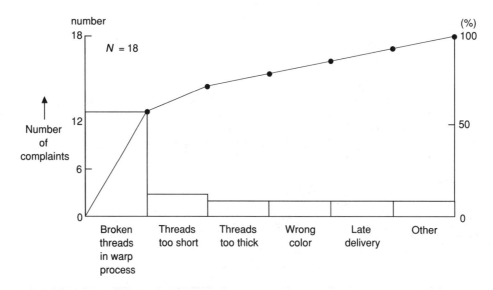

**Figure 12-8.  Pareto Chart of Complaints**

## Establishing Objectives

Between April and September of 1984 the average number of broken warp threads was 11 broken threads per 1,000 warp threads, 10,000 yards long. (See Figure 12-9.) We determined to reduce this number to 6 broken threads per 1,000 threads per 1,000 yards by March 1985.

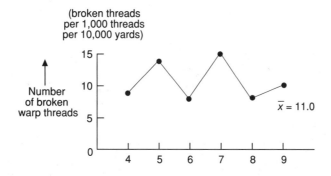

**Figure 12-9. Time Sequence of Number of Broken Warp Threads**

## Understanding Current Circumstances

*Understanding causes.* See Figure 12-10.

*Making a Pareto chart of causes of broken warp threads.* The largest cause of broken warp threads was slubs (places where the thread is unusually thick and catches in the equipment). Because the causes of the broken threads in the user's side have to do with both slubs and individual thread tensile strength, we included both of these factors in our analysis. (See Figure 12-11)

## Analysis of Causes

1. We constructed the statistical distribution of Figure 12-12 to see what kind of relationship individual thread tensile strength has with broken warp threads. (The individual thread tensile strength was measured by the user while the work was in progress.)
   • The result showed a significance to the 1 percent level. Consequently, we can say that there is a strong correlation between individual thread tensile strength and the number of broken warp threads.
2. Next, we constructed a statistical distribution to see what kind of relationship water content of the threads has with tensile strength. (See Figure 12-13.)
   • The result was a correlation significant to the 1 percent level. Consequently, we can say that there is a strong correlation between water content and individual thread tensile strength.

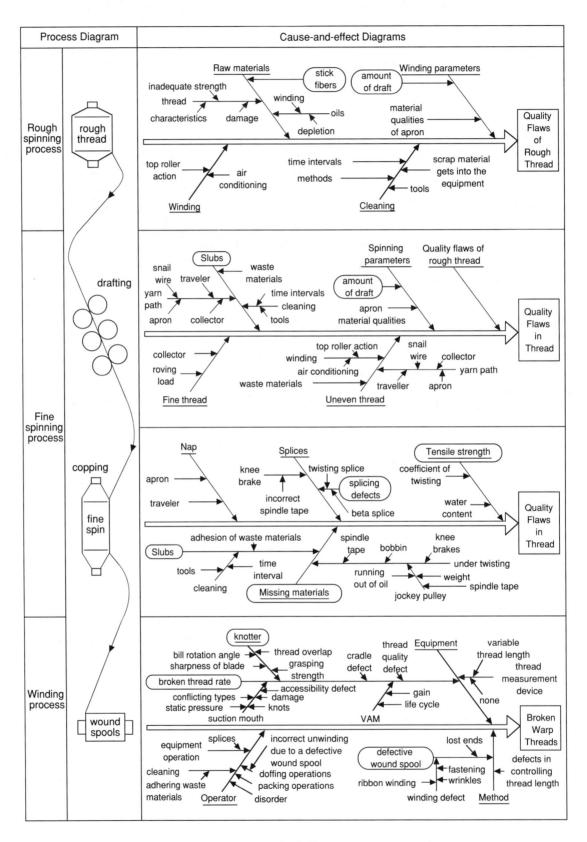

**Figure 12-10.  Cause-and-effect Diagrams for Each Process**

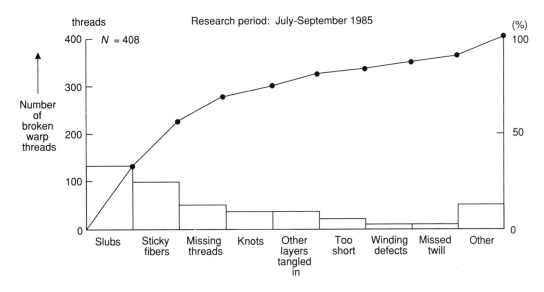

**Figure 12-11. Pareto Chart of the Causes of Broken Warp Threads**

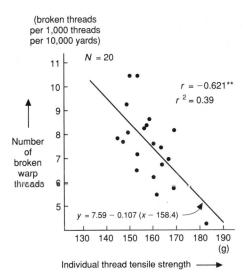

**Figure 12-12. Scatter Diagram of Individual Thread Tensile Strength and Number of Broken Warp Threads**

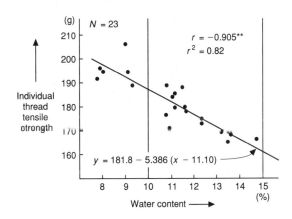

**Figure 12-13. Scatter Diagram of Water Content of Threads and Individual Thread Tensile Strength**

3. We concluded that through regular control of the water content of the threads, we can track their tensile strength. Figure 12-14 shows the chart used for controlling the water content of the thread.
   - At group number 20 (point 1) we implemented action to bring down the water content.
   - At group number 26 (point 2) we ceased the action.
4. The thickness of the thread is also related to the individual thread tensile strength. Because of this we performed tests on the elongation factors of the fine spinning process to reduce the amount of variability in thread thickness. (Elongation $A$ is the current process; elongation $B$ is the test process.)
   - The difference between the two populations was significant to the 1 percent level. Consequently, we can say that the weight dispersion in the case of elongation factor $B$ is smaller then the dispersing in the case of elongation factor $A$. We changed from elongation factor $A$ to elongation factor $B$. (See Figure 12-15.)
5. To quantify how splicing thread reduces its tensile strength, we compared the strength of spliced thread with that of regular thread. (See Figure 12-16.)
   - The averages of the two populations were calculated to have a difference significant to the 1 percent level. Consequently, we can say that the tensile strength of spliced thread is considerably lower than that of normal thread.
   - Of the splices in threads, 45 percent are caught during the winding process. The rest of the splices are not removed, and it is thought that the ensuing slubs result in broken threads in the warping process because they get caught in the equipment. If the operations are done following the standard operating procedures, then the splices are removed during the winding process. We are performing checks to ensure that the splicing is being performed according to standards.
6. To further reduce the number of slubs, we equipped the coarse spinning machine in the coarse spinning process with a slider, and measured the change in slubs caused by crash mat defects. (See Figure 12-17.)
   - The results of hypothesis testing large, medium, and small crash mat defects on the population of defects showed a 5 percent significance for all three of them. Consequently, we can say that the installation of the slider reduced large, medium, and small crash mat defects.

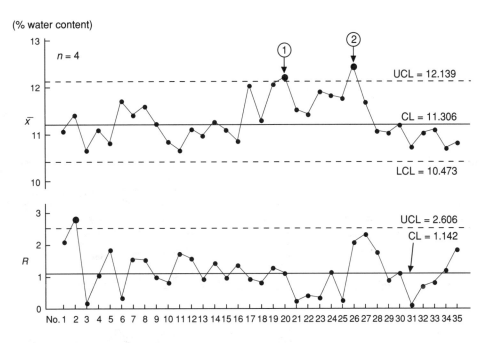

**Figure 12-14. x̄-R Control Chart of Water Content of Threads**

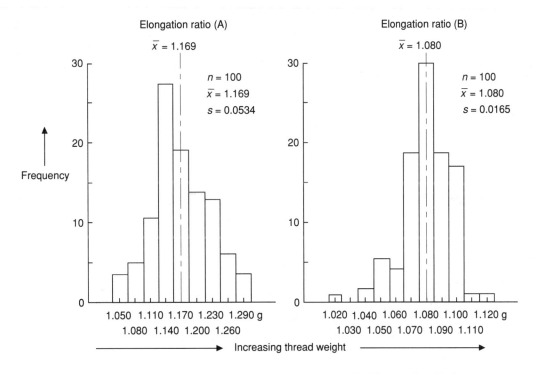

**Figure 12-15. Histograms of Thread Weight in Processes with Elongation Ratios of (A) and (B)**

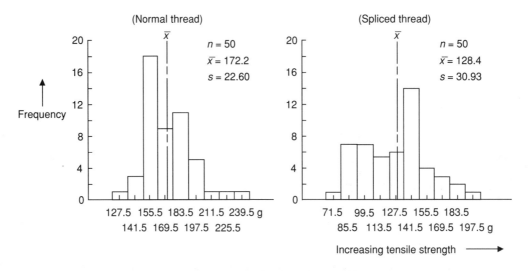

**Figure 12-16.  Histograms of Tensile Strengths of Normal and Spliced Thread**

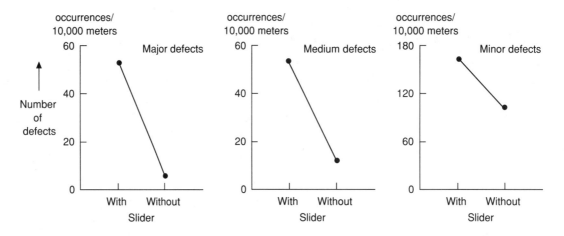

**Figure 12-17.  Defects with and without the Slider**

## Results of Analysis and Action

1.  There is a strong correlation between the individual thread tensile strength and the number of broken threads, and also between the water content of the threads and the single thread tensile strength. We are performing daily control on the water content of the threads using an $\bar{x}$-R control chart.

2. When it comes to the elongation ratio in the fine spinning process, ratio *B* yields less variability than ratio *A* in the thickness of the thread. Consequently, we changed the elongation ratio from the current value of *A* to the new value of *B*.
3. Because spliced thread has lower tensile strength than normal thread, and because when the splices are not eliminated during the winding process they lead to broken threads during the warping process, we are performing checks and instructions in the standard splicing operations to eliminate splices from the winding process.
4. Because the slider reduces the number of large, medium, and small crash mat defects, we are using the slider.

## Verifying Results

See Figures 12-18 and 12-19.

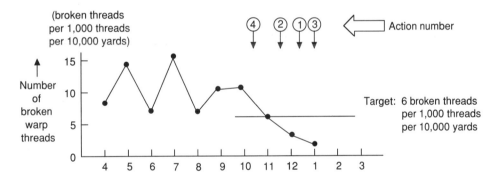

Figure 12-18. Changes in Numbers of Broken Warp Threads

## Where to Go from Here

1. Control the sticking fibers.
2. Begin a corrective action dealing with missing threads, starting with addressing slubs and tensile strength.
3. Work to reduce the number of broken threads in the warping process by relating them to broken thread rates in the winding process.

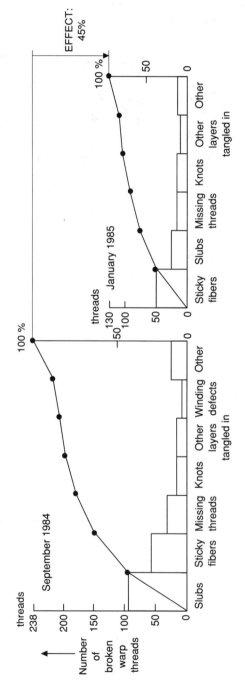

**Figure 12-19.  Pareto Chart of Causes of Broken Warp Threads**

# 13

# Effective Problem Solving in the Procurement Department

## PURCHASING AND CONTRACTING

Procurement is buying necessary raw materials, equipment, and tools for manufacturing activities. Depending on the number and nature of products being procured, the definition can be divided into *purchasing* and *contracting*.

*Purchasing* is procuring from other companies manufactured products and raw materials that are based on the designs of the other companies. The attributes, measurements, and quality levels are determined mostly by the seller. An example of this type of activity is purchasing through catalog sales.

*Contracting* is procuring from other companies manufactured products that are based on designs supplied by the buyer company and manufactured at the request of the buyer company. It refers to the procurement of parts that are made to the unique specifications of the buyer, or to the subcontracting of certain portions of the manufacturing process.

In some companies the distinction is not drawn between purchasing and contracting, and both activities are handled by the same department. In many companies, however, purchasing is done by the purchasing or materials department, while contracting is done by the contract management department or manufacturing department.

## THE FUNCTION OF PROCUREMENT

Called the "third profitability source department," the procurement department aims to "buy adeptly." "Buying adeptly" is not just "beating down the prices" of the raw materials or parts it purchases at the request of the manufacturing department or other groups.

The procurement department must systematically cooperate with the manufacturing, engineering, planning, accounting, and other departments on strategies to make products inexpensively. In terms of the quality assurance sequence, the procurement department doesn't step in once a product reaches the manufacturing stage. Rather, the procurement department must participate also in the product development, design, prototyping, and production preparation stages and must make assertive recommendations on sourcing, vendors, raw materials and parts, and so forth.

The procurement department plays four important roles: selecting vendors, establishing purchase prices, ensuring required qualities, and ensuring quantities and delivery.

## Selecting Vendors

Selection of vendors is the most important task of the procurement department, and the foremost concern in favorable procurement. If an excellent vendor is selected, then quality and delivery schedules are certain and it is possible to purchase the materials or parts at agreeable prices.

When selecting vendors, the procurement department must work closely with the engineering, design, inspection, and manufacturing departments to evaluate the technical abilities, equipment capabilities and capacities, level of quality control, financial state, management policies and direction, and other qualifications of the potential vendors.

An overview of the vendor is first provided through use of a vendor audit form such as the one shown in Table 13-1. Checklists are then used to obtain numeric scores for objective evaluation.

## Establishing Purchase Prices

Low purchase prices are not necessarily "good." For example, when you are negotiating a long-term purchase agreement, you must consider the long-term stability of the supply, understand the supplier's cost structure, and work to establish the most appropriate price.

It is recommended that scientific methods such as value analysis (VA) and purchase cost standards (PCS) be used when establishing purchase prices.

**Table 13-1. Vendor Audit Form (Example)**

Industrial Survey Card

| Type of Industry: | | Category No.: |
|---|---|---|

| Company Name: | Address/Phone: | Administrative/ Office Address: |
|---|---|---|
| | | Contact Person/Phone: |

| Capitalization: | Date Established: | Monthly Sales Volume: | Monthly Operating Profit: |
|---|---|---|---|

Factory Names:

(Circle the factory responsible for the product in question)

| Special characteristics of the company (Itemize quality aspects, technical aspects, etc.): | Sales volume, structure, and percentages: | Product/percent of sales: | Major suppliers: |
|---|---|---|---|

| Industrial ranking: (Market share and competitors in industry) | Products purchased from the company: | (Product names, purchasing volumes, etc.) |
|---|---|---|

| Management policies and direction (hoshin) : | Products sold to the company: | (Product names, production capabilities, etc.) |
|---|---|---|

| Selling points of the company: | Production control system for the product in question: | (Production planning, process changes, etc.) |
|---|---|---|

| Production process flow: | Smallest production lot: |
|---|---|
| | Smallest delivery lot: |
| | Shortest lead time: |
| | Inventory capacity (products): |
| | Engineering development Complaint handling AM systems: |
| | Sales system (organization, number of personnel, etc.): |

### Ensuring Required Qualities

The procurement department has the responsibility of purchasing materials and parts that match the qualities required by the engineering and design departments. To do this, the procurement department must request that the engineering department specifically and quantitatively express their requirements and that suppliers deliver products that conform to the specifications. In some cases, it must provide direct guidance to the vendors. A crucial role of the procurement department is obtaining low prices while ensuring suitable quality.

### Ensuring Quantities and Delivery

Delivery and inventory systems such as the *kanban* system and *just-in-time* delivery have recently become major topics for procurement departments. Another major role of the procurement department is to ensure the purchase of just the right amount of goods at the time when they are needed.

The procurement department must establish order amounts and delivery times after considering many things — the order quantities on the purchaser's side, the lot size on the supplier's side, the supplier's lead time, the average inventory amount of inventory, the space available for inventory and carrying costs, methods and lag times for transportation, the frequency of orders, the cost to place an order, and so forth.

When delivery dates or order volumes change for the convenience of the purchaser, or when, on the other hand, there are delays because of circumstances on the supplier's side, then the procurement department must quickly act to correct the problem.

## DEFINING PROCUREMENT POLICIES AND DIRECTION (HOSHIN)

Because often in procurement departments each individual buyer negotiates with vendors to establish terms and agreements, there is a danger that the teamwork of the buyers will degenerate into individual play. To guard against this, each company should clearly establish a set of procurement policies, and then make and execute plans based upon these policies.

Some companies include fundamental purchasing philosophy in these policies, while others even include specific directions for purchasing activities. An overview of the purchasing policy of company *A* follows.

1. The procurement department aims to purchase objects of the correct quality at the correct time, in the appropriate volumes, and at the lowest price.
2. The procurement department exercises complete lead time management on raw materials for a reduction of inventory, and works to shorten procurement lead times.
3. The procurement department strives to collect data from the market, providing the engineering and manufacturing departments with information on new materials while profitably obtaining market-leading commodities.
4. Because the vendor is also a party that cooperates in the manufacturing activities of the company, rather than adhering to an unconditional principle of purchasing the least expensive goods, the procurement department will create improved relations with the vendors.

When creating a specific policy and direction for execution, the following items must be defined:

***Internal sourcing versus external sourcing.*** The supply of materials or products can be made in-house (internal sourcing) or purchased from outside (external sourcing).

Usually, the decision on what type of sourcing to use is made based on comparisons of overall costs and profitability, with consideration given to the decisive elements of the company's technical abilities, equipment capabilities, personnel, and so on. However, when company managers decide what must be made in-house and what must be purchased externally, they must first consider the following:

1. Cost comparisons: current costs and forecast costs
2. Excess equipment and human capacity, and use rates
3. Required technological and quality control levels, and the existence of technological secrets
4. The lead times involved in the procurement of materials and parts
5. Inventory levels, inventory space, and transportation costs

*Procuring from affiliated companies versus open procurement.* Recently, many companies have created supplier companies or have affiliated with the companies from which they purchase or with which they contract. Yet many companies still espouse the principle of free economic competition, choosing vendors freely in an open purchasing system.

The benefit of the affiliate purchasing system is that with a fixed group of contractors, it is easy to procure items of the necessary quality at the necessary time, and to do so fairly economically. Ensuring quality and delivery is a major objective.

Open purchasing means searching for products that fulfill company requirements in terms of quality, cost, and delivery — on the open market. The open market system has great merit for the purchase of materials, JIS products, or general commodity market goods. However, when the company requires unique specifications or an especially severe quality, then the number of suitable vendors is limited and the delivery requirements may be hard to meet.

*Centralized purchasing versus satellite purchasing.* Although there are many ways to organize purchasing departments depending on the size of company, the type of industry, and the administrative system, in any sort of system the purchasing department works on either a centralized, company-wide system or a satellite, factory-specific system.

If the purchase volume is very high, or if the entire company is using the same materials, or if the supplier is a major player in the field, then it is probably most profitable if the top management of both companies make connections with each other in a centralized purchasing system. Such a system is also beneficial when a company wants access to the newest technological information of the supplier.

On the other hand, if the price of the goods is relatively low, if the goods ordered are based on complicated drawings or specifications, if the products required are regional goods, or if there are urgent time constraints, then it is profitable to use a factory-level procurement system.

When drafting standards for decision-making on centralized satellite purchasing, consider as criteria not only efficiency but also the importance of creating smooth relations with vendors.

## PROBLEM AREAS IN PROCUREMENT DEPARTMENTS, AND WAYS TO RESOLVE THEM

Table 13-2 shows problem areas typical of procurement departments, and hints for their resolution.

Table 13-3 shows the research themes adopted by the 135 participants of the Thirteenth Quality Control Seminar for Procurement and Materials Departments, sponsored by JUSE. It serves as a good source of information on the types of problems being faced on a daily basis by those in charge of procurement and materials departments. However, themes pertaining to the issues that purchasing agents are most concerned about — costs — are few. This probably reflects the orientation of the themes to presentation in seminars outside of the purchasing agents' own companies.

## AN EXAMPLE OF PROBLEM SOLVING IN A PROCUREMENT DEPARTMENT

The following examples show problem-solving activities for the theme "Reducing late deliveries of purchased parts for kerosene water heaters."

### Reason for Selection of Theme

Company $N$ is a manufacturer of household water heaters. It contracts for all of the major components of the water heaters, performing only the assembly process in-house. This theme, therefore, was adopted as a means of controlling materials to stabilize the in-house production processes, and to eliminate late deliveries of the products to the users.

### Understanding Current Circumstances

We investigated the number of late deliveries of parts for use in the kerosene water heaters. (See Figure 13-1.) For this we determined that late deliveries of the pressed parts and the burners ordered from companies $A$, $B$, and $C$ were the most severe.

**Table 13-2. Problem Areas in the Procurement Department, and Ways to Resolve Them**

| Functions | Issues | Hints for Resolution |
|---|---|---|
| Selection of vendors | market surveys | demand, trends, characteristics of the industry, business practices |
| | development of new vendors | management policies and direction, financial state of company, technical abilities |
| | defining requirements to do business | payment schedules, payment method |
| | leading and nurturing suppliers | participation in capital, affiliations, cooperatives |
| Establishing purchase prices | understanding the raw materials, market conditions | sources of data (trade sheets, stock market reports) |
| | establishing standard costs | production process flows, standard labor contents, basic units |
| | establishing order volumes and production lots | smallest production lots, order amounts, smallest delivery units |
| | making cost reduction plans | reducing the labor contents, VA activities, PCS |
| Ensuring demanded qualities | defining purchased goods quality standards | purchased goods, quality specification documents, approval drawings |
| | securing quality assurance contracts | quality assurance periods, assurance detail |
| | providing quality assurance leadership to external suppliers | QC education, standardization, incoming inspections |
| Ensuring volumes and delivery schedules | establishing lead times | lead times for each part or material, longest lead time |
| | standardizing of the ordering system | order forms, delivery forms, receipt verification |
| | making mid-length unofficial plans | yearly order quantities, amounts necessary for each month, informal strategy |
| | establishing appropriate inventory levels | inventory locations, inventory capacity, minimal inventory levels |
| Procurement management tasks | establishing purchasing policies | long-range policy and direction, yearly policy and direction, action items |
| | streamlining payment work | computerization |
| | defining vendor evaluation criteria | evaluation items, evaluation frequency, award system |

Problem areas in the procurement department

**Table 13-3.  Research Themes Presented in the 13th Quality Control Seminar for Procurement and Materials Departments**

| Category | Examples of Themes | Number of themes |
|---|---|---|
| Delivery | • Reducing late deliveries<br>• Shortening procurement lead times<br>• Improving ratios of deliveries made on specified day | 40 (30 themes) |
| Quality | • Improving defect rates in parts and incoming inspections<br>• Improving quality in new products<br>• Performing external vendor quality control | 32 (24 themes) |
| Office work | • Raising efficiency of the work involved in ordering<br>• Improving the management of purchasing budgets<br>• Reducing problems by defining contract requirements | 29 (21 themes) |
| Inventory | • Reducing inventories of principal raw materials<br>• Improving stock turn rates<br>• Reducing discrepancies in on-shelf parts inventories | 17 (13 themes) |
| Vendors | • Making correct evaluations of vendors based on vendor evaluation forms<br>• Providing direction for vendors through QCD evaluations<br>• Improving the control methods of suppliers | 9 (7 themes) |
| Cost | • Reducing costs through using VA<br>• Promoting profitable purchasing practices by creating competitive relationships<br>• Reducing costs by using B-grade products | 8 (6 themes) |

$N = 135$.
The parenthesized numbers indicate a normalized index of number of themes in the category per 100 themes.

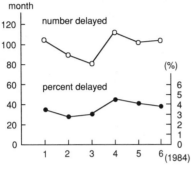
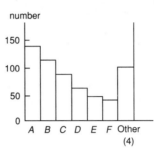
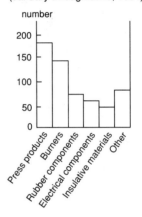

**Figure 13-1.  Number of Delayed Deliveries**

## Establishing Objectives

Two objectives were established:

- Number of late deliveries: Reducing the current level of late deliveries (from January to June, 1984) from 97 to 50 (by 31 December 1984)
- Percentage of deliveries late: Reducing the current level of 3.4 percent to 1.7 percent

## Analysis of Causes

We visited companies *A, B,* and *C,* discussed with them the causes of their troubles with late deliveries, and analyzed the causes of late deliveries in the past. (See Figure 13-2 and Table 13-4.)

## Corrective Action Plan

We picked up the most important cause factors from the cause-and-effect diagram, and devised specific improvement plans. (See Figure 13-3.) We also defined a system that includes communication between the contractors and the

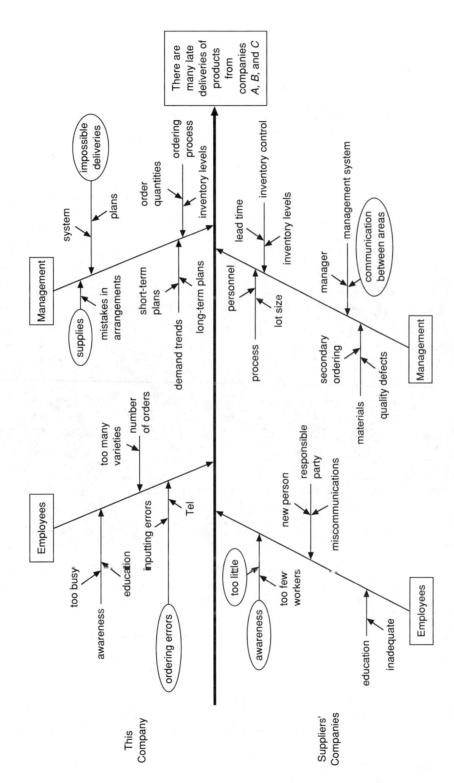

**Figure 13-2. Cause-and-effect Diagram of Delayed Deliveries**

related departments (materials, sales, production control groups) in our company. This system takes the form of *sales plan* to *production plan* to *orders to contractor* to *processing* to *delivery*. (See Figure 13-4.)

**Table 13-4.  Number of Delayed Deliveries Attributable to Each Cause**
**(Total between January and June, 1984)**

| | | A Co. | B Co. | C Co. | Total Delayed Deliveries | Total Percentage Delayed Deliveries |
|---|---|---|---|---|---|---|
| Caused by this company | Impossible delivery schedules | 25 | 30 | 20 | 75 | 22.7 |
| | Ordering errors | 8 | 10 | 10 | 28 | 8.5 |
| | Late goods | 5 | 0 | 3 | 8 | 2.4 |
| | Other | 10 | 5 | 7 | 22 | 6.7 |
| Caused by the supplier company | Process delays caused by lack of awareness | 45 | 15 | 25 | 85 | 25.8 |
| | Communication problems within the company | 15 | 35 | 12 | 62 | 18.8 |
| | Second-level supplier quality problems | 10 | 5 | 5 | 20 | 6.1 |
| | Other | 12 | 10 | 8 | 30 | 9.1 |
| Total | | 130 | 110 | 90 | 330 | 100 |

| Problem Area | Specific Improvement Plan | Responsibility Our Company | Responsibility Supplier |
|---|---|---|---|
| Impossible delivery schedules | Clarify the production system (with an unofficial 3-month production plan) | O | |
| | Reexamine inventory items and levels | O | |
| Ordering Errors | Determine parties who should be contacted | O | |
| | Strictly observe written orders | O | |
| Process delays caused by a lack of awareness | Educate each process leader | | O |
| | Install a control ledger | | O |
| Supplier companies' in-house communication problems | Clearly define communication systems | | O |
| | Keep a log of people responsible for processes | | O |
| Inadequate quality of goods from secondary suppliers | Introduce QC to secondary suppliers | O | |

**Figure 13-3.  Specific Improvements**

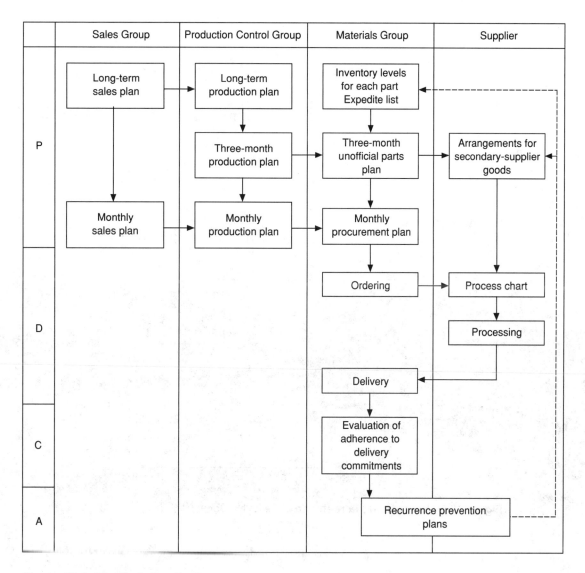

**Figure 13-4. The Ordering System**

## Verifying Results

Through the cooperation between our company and each of the contractors in the execution of specific improvement plans, by December 1984 we had cleared both of our initial goals: reducing the number of late deliveries and reducing the percentage of late deliveries. (See Figures 13-5 and 13-6.)

## Anti-backslide Measures

We performed standardization by creating and revising the following types of standards:

1. Unofficial documents and ordering summaries
2. Parts procurement delivery management summaries
3. Vendor evaluation criteria and the like

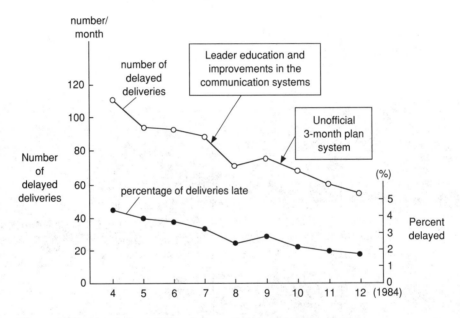

**Figure 13-5.  Number and Percentage of Delayed Deliveries**

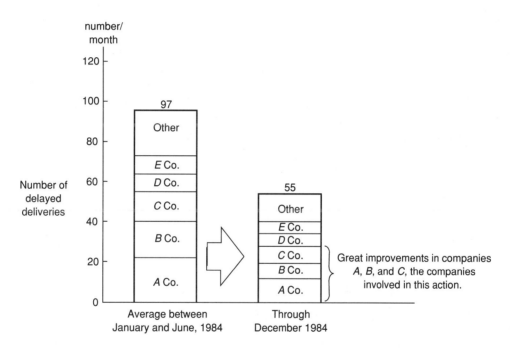

**Figure 13-6.  Delayed Deliveries per Supplier Company**

# 14
# Effective Problem Solving in the Sales and Service Departments

The role of the sales and service departments — the departments that directly contact the consumers — is essential to the company's continued business of economically developing, designing, manufacturing, testing, selling, and servicing products that satisfy consumers. Although there is a tendency to neglect QC activities in sales departments, this is partially because of the prevailing belief among sales personnel that *quality* means *product quality* and has little bearing on their own work.

As Chapter 2 discussed, the word *quality* means both

- the quality of products, and
- the quality of job performances.

Thus, the interpretation of quality is not limited to the quality of products but also includes the quality of service and the quality of job performance. Therefore, the fundamental role of the sales and service departments should be to improve the quality of the job performance and the service in the sales and service work, as well as selling the product.

## THE FUNCTION OF THE SALES AND SERVICE DEPARTMENTS

Although the roles of the sales and service departments probably vary according to type of industry, product line, and sales channels, the major functions of most sales and service departments are the following.

101

## Setting Sales Targets

To achieve target sales levels set at the beginning of the period, sales managers usually make yearly plans or monthly itineraries, comparing the plans to actual results using daily or weekly reports, analyzing causes and effects for the period, and then taking some sort of action. These actions are all vital to QC. In many cases sales targets cannot be achieved solely through reliance on past methods, and it becomes necessary to devise and implement new strategies. Managers must improve channels in existing markets and mobilize customer visit activities, or they must perform market expansion campaigns, for example. However, there are also many times when emphasis is placed on the opening of entirely new markets; in such cases, sales locations must be established, product flows must be studied, and the requirements of the customers must be understood. Although the control items for these functions might include sales volumes, growth rates (compared with the previous year), the number of new accounts, market share, and so forth, we recommend that each of these factors be understood and controlled through stratification by sales campaign, market, sales location, salesman, and so forth.

## Creating a Sales Plan

To create a high-accuracy sales plan, you must estimate demand through use of various forecasting methods. However, the basis for these activities is found in analysis of the data of the previous year's actual sales results; for this, effective statistical methods need to be employed. Although historical data provide much information about the future, they do not constitute a reliable forecasting method. This is because data from the past are often unclear, and thus the credibility of each individual datum is lacking. Because of this, you should review the data being collected day to day and question the purpose for which the information is being collected and its possible applications. While data collection should certainly be based on 5W1H, and while the data should be stratified, keep in mind that the results of data analysis should show what factors are meaningful and what factors are not in a constantly changing sea of characteristics. Thus data should show differences between products, between channels, between sales locations, and between sales campaigns; differences before and after changes in management systems; the effects of other companies' trends; and any changes in the market environment.

The basic formula for making sales forecasts is:

Sales forecast =
estimated aggregate demand for a particular item ×
market share of the applicable company

Consequently, to make a highly accurate sales forecast, you must first have an accurate estimate of aggregate demand and an accurate understanding of the company's market share. Various methods have been developed for estimating aggregate demand. Time series regression analysis, time series scatter analysis, and exponential smoothing are examples. In recent years multiple regression analysis, multivariate analysis, and quantification methods have also come to be used as effective forecasting tools.

## Understanding Market Trends and Feeding Data Back into Product Planning

By understanding precisely what the users are demanding and by analyzing market trends, a company can introduce, at the right time, products that are different from those of their competitors. Market, customer, and sales data are fed to the product planning and development departments. To create an essential system of feedback, a company should reexamine the following points about the existing system.

1. Do the users understand, and are they satisfied with, the target functions of the current products?
2. Are user complaints and grievances listened to positively, with none "falling through the cracks?"

Problem areas can be discovered through constant feedback, as a part of the sales activities, of these two points into improvements in existing products, and through regular checks on whether quality data are being used in the development of new products for the subsequent period or year.

## Performing Quality Assurance Activities in the Sales and Service Stage

Although this function is tied to the previous one, the marketing department should engage in quality assurance activities before the actual sales activities begin. It does this by ensuring the completeness of product lines being offered through catalogs and so forth, holding press conferences to announce products, and ensuring adequate PR to the users, explaining the products' features in terms of quality. Activities by which sales personnel can publicize to users the differences between the new product and previous products by the same company or differences between the new product and products by competitors are especially important.

On the other hand, when troubles arise in products that have already been sold, after-service must be performed without delay. Sitting for days on complaint data without taking action is unforgivable. In complete customer orientation, the details of complaints must be studied, quick action taken, and recurrence prevention strategies put in place. Of course, to proactively circumvent complaints, sales and service personnel must make regular visits to customers to study user satisfaction levels and understand the actual circumstances in which the product is used.

## PROBLEM AREAS IN SALES AND SERVICE DEPARTMENTS, AND WAYS TO RESOLVE THEM

Table 14-1 shows the major problem areas in the four functions of sales and service departments, and lists hints for their resolution.

## AN EXAMPLE OF PROBLEM SOLVING IN THE SALES DEPARTMENT

The following example of problem solving in a sales department, "Raising the market share of product A," is a summary of a report by Yoshito Tomita (Nikka Whiskey Sales Department), from the December 1983 issue of *Engineers* magazine (published by JUSE). This is an example of deployment of sales activities in branch X to recover market share three years after the release of product A. It is also an example of success in raising the market share of product A by examining the variability in outlet coverage rates through stratified results of the 472 outlets in the territory, and through operations analysis centering on the sales visits. This is a valuable improvement activity report showing just how important it is to accurately analyze actual circumstances and correctly understand problem areas.

**Table 14-1.  Problem Areas in Sales and Service Departments, and Ways to Resolve Them**

| Functions | Problem Areas | Hints for Resolution |
|---|---|---|
| Achieving sales targets | Monthly sales levels do not reach targets. | Compare the actual sales results with the target values according to each of the stratified cause factors below and find the variance from target for each. Stratify according to salesperson, sales route, outlets, sales strategies, sales regions, product types, number of sales calls made, trends in other companies, areas, and so forth.<br><br>For example, make a matrix of types of products and routes and compare actual results to targets in each cell.<br><br> |
|  | New-market development isn't progressing. | Research the product distribution flows and understand the working of competing products while learning the conditions of the customers.  Show the product flows of similar products using a flow chart, and for each point in the flow chart write requirements for success such as key person, and so forth.<br><br>For example, make a chart of the activities being done to develop each new customer; study an activities review document showing the activities that have succeeded in developing new customers in the past, that have failed, and so forth.<br><br>State of Activities Overview Table<br><br><table><tr><th>Name of New Customer Being Developed</th><th>Number of Visits</th><th>Do We Know Who Key Person Is?</th><th>Contacts Made with Key Person?</th><th>Other Companies' Actions</th><th>•••</th></tr><tr><td>A</td><td>5</td><td>YES</td><td>2</td><td>•••</td><td>•••</td></tr><tr><td>B</td><td>0</td><td>NO</td><td>0</td><td>•••</td><td>•••</td></tr><tr><td>C</td><td>1</td><td>NO</td><td>0</td><td>•••</td><td>•••</td></tr><tr><td>D</td><td>2</td><td>NO</td><td>0</td><td>•••</td><td>•••</td></tr></table> |

**Table 14-1.  (Continued)**

| Functions | Problem Areas | Hints for Resolution |
|---|---|---|
| | Sales and market shares are not increasing. | It is probably difficult to increase sales and market shares for all products at once.  Narrow in on principal products and manage on the basis of priorities.  It is especially important that the efficiency of the sales activities be raised so that they do not become too diffuse.  Because it is possible for the market share to fall even while sales levels are rising (i.e., when the market is growing faster than the company's sales), both topics — increasing sales and increasing market share — should be addressed simultaneously.<br><br>While of course the movement of other companies should be tracked, understand each of their products in terms of Q, C, and D separately.<br><br>Our company  ○ Previous period  ● This period<br>Competitor  □ Previous period  ■ This period<br><br>Market share / Sales volume<br>■ Competitor<br>□ — ○ target<br>○ — ● actual results<br>} analyze the variance |
| Creating sales plans | The accuracy of sales forecasts is poor, so sales do not increase. | Establish target values when devising sales plans by performing scientific, methodic studies using demand forecasting methods and statistical methods.  Closely examine the movements of data in the past, and define the background for the selection of target levels.<br><br>Set target values for each product, route, sales representative, sales method, and so forth.<br><br>Use the method of moving averages, the method of exponential smoothing, multiple regression techniques, and the quantification methods.<br><br>At this time the variability of the data should be carefully considered, and estimates of upper and lower limits of reliability ratios should be established and rechecked. |
| | The sales plan and the production plan aren't synchronized. | Begin by understanding the system by which the production plan is established, and then reexamine the relationship of this system to the sales system to see if they work together smoothly.<br><br>Along with accurately understanding the time lags between the receipt of orders and the delivery of those orders, create a system in which information about changes in sales plans or production plans are quickly communicated to the other departments through a manufacturing/sales communication meeting.<br><br>Estimate one month's sales by reviewing the results from the previous month along with the tactics used that month.  Adjust the expenditure plan, adjust the priorities of the various sales locations, their targets, and so forth, and then reconcile between sales, production, and warehousing.  Ensure cooperation in meetings between these functional groups. |

| Functions | Problem Areas | Hints for Resolution |
|---|---|---|
| Creating sales plans (cont'd.) | Because of the lack of certainty about actual inventory levels, prompt delivery systems cannot be established. | Research the actual conditions of the inventory at supplier locations, distribution centers, outlets, the home company, etc., and create an inventory plan for each product.<br><br>While creating a supply system that conforms to regional requirements, implement an on-line computer system to reconcile the inventories in each inventory point. |
| Understanding market trends and feeding data back to product planning | The competitor's strategy is not fully understood. | Visit the various sales channels (outlets, small stores, etc.) and make close connections with the key persons from whom data can be collected.<br><br>Along with researching and analyzing past strategies deployed by the competitors, pay attention to, and collect data about, trends in related industries. |
| | Data that can used by product planning cannot be obtained, and thus cannot be applied to the market. | Work to extract latent complaints from the market instead of just analyzing data about complaints that are made to the company.<br><br>While performing service, listen to the customers to collect data about whether the service system is fulfilling the needs of the customers.<br><br>Examine the number of cases when complaint information has been used in product improvements, and the degree to which it has been used. Perform comparisons with the products of other companies based on information collected from the users. |
| Performing quality assurance during the sale and service stage | The rules for dealing with market complaints are not clearly defined. | Clarify the complaint handling system. To do this, establish what the flow of information will be. Take the responsibility to provide feedback to the involved departments, and to also pass data back to the users. Also collect data such as the time it takes to handle complaints and the level of complaint resolution to evaluate the promptness of complaint servicing.<br><br>Use system diagrams and other methods to clearly define the complaint handling system, clearly record the responsible departments (parties), the necessary conferences and meetings, and the management materials for each step.<br><br>Track and graph the number of complaints, complaint recurrence rates, time to handle complaints, number of complaints per product, complaints for new vs. existing products, and other data. |

## Reason for Selection of Theme

Sales of product *A* had begun three years ago but during the previous year the market share held by the product began to fall. Of the 16 branches across the country, the reduction in sales seen in branch *X* was the most remarkable. Although an immediate counteraction was attempted through a special sale with bonus premiums, there were no significant results. The decision was made to identify the fundamental causes of the reduced market share and then to research strategies to raise market share of product *A* in sales branch *X*.

## Understanding Current Circumstances and Analysis

*Changes in market share of product* **A.** As Figure 14-1 shows, the market share held by product *A* began to fall in the beginning of 1982. The bonus premium sale had no effects, and by the beginning of 1983 there were still no leads as to how to recover the market share. The sales volume in sales branch *X*, as shown in Figure 14-2, had especially fallen; its January to April sales volume was only 88 percent of the sales recorded for the same period in the previous year, as compared with the national average for the same comparison of 103 percent. Determined to find the causes of these problems, we began a study of the sales conditions in the market for product *A*.

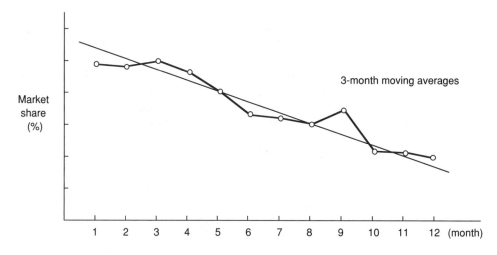

**Figure 14-1. Market Share Movement of Product *A* (Nationally)**

*Product* **A** *market study.* We categorized the outlets according to their sizes and investigated the coverage rates for each category. As is shown in Table 14-2, there was a large difference in coverage rates between our product and the competitors' product in the small outlets. When we further divided these small outlets into three rankings according to size, we discovered that we had only 8 percent coverage in the 85 class C outlets. We also discovered that the competitors' coverage was the same across all of the categories.

*Product coverage rates and sales shares.* We made a graph of the relationships between the coverage rates and sales shares of several similar products, including product *A*. As is shown in Figure 14-3, the relationship formed a truncated parabola. Through this graph we knew that in order to raise our mar-

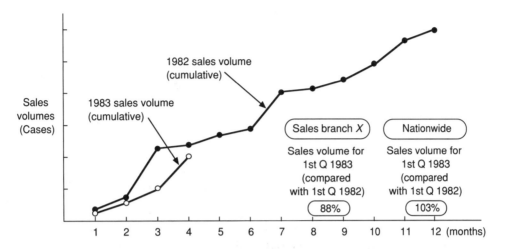

**Figure 14-2. Sales of Product A in Sales Branch X**

**Table 14-2. Product Coverage Rates in Outlets**

| Store Size | Number of Stores | Product A | Competing Goods |
|---|---|---|---|
| | | (%) | (%) |
| Large | 13 | 69 | 85 |
| Mid-size | 78 | 47 | 87 |
| Small | 381 | (26) | (84) |
| Total | 472 | 47 (mean) | 85 (mean) |

| Small Stores | Number of Stores | Product A | Competing Goods |
|---|---|---|---|
| | | (%) | (%) |
| A-ranked | 76 | 42 | 82 |
| B-ranked | 220 | 27 | 87 |
| C-ranked | 85 | (8) | 76 |
| Total | 381 | 26 (mean) | 84 (mean) |

ket share we would need to have at least 80 percent coverage. We drew up the cause-and-effect diagram shown in Figure 14-4 to analyze the causes of the low coverage rates of product A. From the results, we selected the most common problems found in sales branch X:

- The frequency of visits to the liquor outlets is too low.
- There is no follow-up with the liquor stores.
- The visits are not distributed equally to all liquor stores.
- There is no standard pertaining to visits to liquor stores.
- The owners of the liquor stores had never tasted product A.

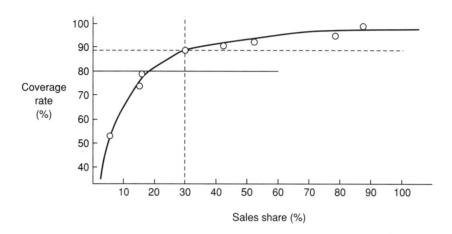

**Figure 14-3.  Product Coverage Rates and Sales Shares**

To summarize, the greatest cause for the low coverage rate of product *A* was inadequate promotion activities aimed at the liquor stores.

***The status of visits to the small liquor stores.*** The results of a study of sales calls to small liquor stores are shown in Table 14-3. It was clear that there was a large gap between the frequency of our visits and the visits of our competitors.

***The relationship between coverage rates and store owners who have tried product* A.**

- Stores where the owners have tried product *A* — 54 percent coverage
- Stores where the owners have not tried product *A* — 23 percent coverage

Also, even in the small class B and class C ranked stores, where the average coverage rates are extremely low, stores that are visited frequently have a 74 percent coverage rate. Furthermore, in stores where the owner has tried product *A*, the coverage rate was an extremely high 83 percent. Consequently, we learned that the stores which carry product *A*, even the small ones, are usually visited frequently by our sales representatives and are very familiar with our product. To increase the number of sales calls by our representatives, we conducted a time-motion analysis.

***The sales representative time-motion analysis.*** We performed a study of the activities of 12 sales representatives, categorizing their actions as sales consultations, office work, transportation, and breaks. The results were that, on the

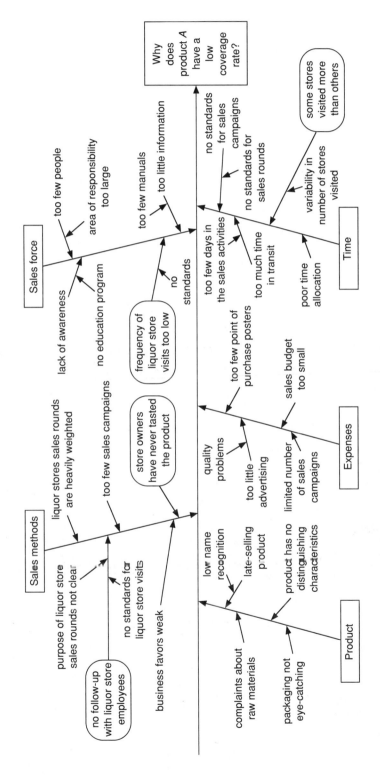

**Figure 14-4. Cause-and-effect Diagram for Low Coverage Rates of Product A**

**Table 14-3.  Comparisons of the Number of Visits to Small Liquor Stores by Our Company vs. Visits by Competitors**

| Small Stores | Number of Stores | Often Visited | | Occasionally Visited | | Rarely Visited | | Total (%) |
|---|---|---|---|---|---|---|---|---|
| | | Us (%) | Competitor (%) | Us (%) | Competitor (%) | Us (%) | Competitor (%) | |
| A-ranked | 76 | 31 | 68 | 30 | 21 | 39 | 11 | 100 |
| B-ranked | 220 | 12 | 46 | 23 | 36 | 65 | 18 | 100 |
| C-ranked | 85 | 1 | 20 | 15 | 33 | 84 | 47 | 100 |
| Total | 381 | 13 | 45 | 23 | 32 | 62 | 23 | 100 |

average, 43 percent the total time was spent in sales consultations; however, there was a large degree of variability in this amount of time, ranging from 27 percent to 59 percent. The "office work" time included ledger work and telephone contacting, and it showed substantial variability among individuals, ranging from 13 percent to 22 percent of the total time.

There were dramatic differences between individuals in terms of time spent in each sales visit and the number of sales visits made per day, and we concluded that there were no clear standards to follow regarding these aspects of the sales work.

## Corrective Action

Based on our analysis of sales activities, we executed the following corrective actions.

In order to raise the market share we must raise our inventory coverage ratios; we adopted the goal of raising the current level of 31 percent to a target level of 80 percent.

We were aware that in order to do this we needed to

- increase the frequency of visits to the small shops,
- have the owners of the shops sample product A,

- make sure that the owners of the shops were informed of the characteristics of product *A*,
- streamline the office work of the sales force and increase the time they spend visiting shops, and
- reduce the amount of variation in time spent in each shop visit.

Aware that such corrective actions are necessary to increase share, we deployed the following programs in the entire sales branch *X* territory in July 1983.

1. We took product literature, in-store point-of-purchase ads, and sample taste kits to the liquor stores to explain the product to potential customers and to allow them to taste it.
2. We reduced dramatically the time the sales force spends in office work, and increased the time spent in sales calls, as well as increasing the number of sales calls.
3. We emphasized direction and education for the sales representatives who have the greatest variability in the their time-motion distributions and who are performing at the lowest levels.

## Results and Anti-backslide Measures

These corrective actions are still in effect today, and the results of the actions are not yet fully understood. However, it is clear that the sales of product *A* in sales branch *X* have improved since the implementation of these programs, and that the growth rates compared to the previous year have improved sharply.

Specifically, although the sales from January to April 1983 were 88 percent (103 percent nationwide) of the sales for the same period the previous year, the same indicator reached 115 percent (104 percent nationwide) for the period after the corrective action began (July to September, 1983).

In other words, whereas before the corrective action sales branch *X* had the worst growth rate nationwide in the company, after the corrective action it had the best. While we think that this will lead to an increase in market share, there is still the need to reverify the relationships with liquor store sales shares and coverage rates, and so on, through another market survey.

Standardization will certainly follow this verification. It is our intention to expand this strategy nationwide, and also to other products.

## Review

Although large parts of this study were done in terms of KKD (*keiken* (experience), *kan* (intuition), and *dokyo* (trial and error) without the benefit of any detailed analyses, through this study we were still able to express current circumstances to some degree quantitatively, and use these quantitative expressions in drawing graphs and charts for graphical analysis, thereby clearly identifying the causes for the troubles and discovering the appropriate corrective actions.

We felt keenly the need to listen closely to the statements of the liquor stores, who are our "next process," raise the frequency of sales calls, and collect as much information as possible in studying corrective action plans.

# 15

# Problem Solving in Assembly Industries

## IMPORTANT POINTS

Many manufacturing operations in assembly industries use production strategies that employ systems such as conveyor-driven assembly lines to manufacture a standardized product. This type of assembly operation is typical in the automobile and household appliance assembly industries. There are also cases, such as in the manufacture of large-scale electrical equipment and prefabricated housing, in which each unit is assembled in the final manufacturing process.

Production lines need to be thoroughly committed to the philosophies of "The next process is the customer" and "Don't let defects reach the next process." Thus work should not continue when there are problems; rather, corrective action should be taken when problems occur, even if it means temporarily stopping the conveyer. If there is no such philosophy, then there will soon be a mountain of defects as well as major rework expenses. To make high-quality products less expensively, it is necessary to simultaneously raise the operation rate of the conveyer line and reduce the defect rates.

Whichever approach is taken, the amount of work done by hand in assembly operations is still great. Although recent developments in robotics have advanced the cause of automation in assembly operations, these operations still center on manual labor. Because of this, and because problem-solving activities in assembly work involve many convoluted human factors, training and education of the operators takes on special significance in the assembly industries. When there are human factors involved in problem-solving activities, the method by which cause-and-effect diagrams are made becomes pivotal.

Furthermore, assembly processes are commonly the last stage in production, collecting many components and parts from previous processes or from vendors. Thus it is essential to make a system for executing incoming inspections and for providing immediate and accurate feedback of quality data to vendors and supplier processes.

## CENTRAL CONCEPTS IN THIS EXAMPLE

As an example of problem-solving activities in assembly we have included a summary of the report "Reducing Electrostatic Discharge (ESD) Damage to Modules in the Card Assembly Process," presented by Shinichi Morikuni of the IBM Japan Nozu Plant, in the presentation meeting of the independent research groups of the 65th JUSE QC Seminar and Basic Course (Osaka).

We think that points such as the following will serve as references.

1. As is shown in the process overview (see Figure 15-1), card assembly is done in a supplier factory, so work on the ESD damage reduction project was done with the supplier factory and the Nozu Factory working in conjunction. As the organization for the promotion of the ESD corrective action, the failure analysis group and the process analysis group each worked on their respective areas of responsibility, and cooperated in systematically addressing the issues, thereby attaining success in the project.

2. Although the complexity of human elements in many assembly operations causes extreme difficulties in making cause-and-effect diagrams, in this case experimental design methods were used to show that factors such as humans, ionizers, and so forth are major cause elements of the operating environments of the various processes wherein static discharge is a problem.

3. Cause-and-effect matrices were made for each process, and an ESD corrective action project that integrated all processes was launched.

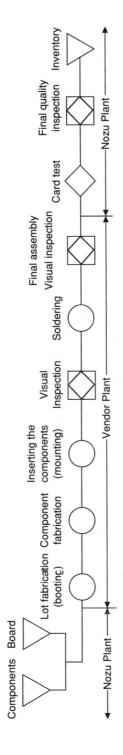

**Figure 15-1. Overview of Card Manufacturing Process**

## THEME:  REDUCING ELECTROSTATIC DISCHARGE (ESD) DAMAGE TO MODULES IN THE CARD ASSEMBLY PROCESS

### Process Overview

See Figure 15-1.

### Reason for Selection of Theme

The problem of electrostatic discharge has recently been addressed several times in the card assembly process, with the result that the number of ESD-related defects has been lowered to less than 10 percent of the defects detected in the card test process. Thus, when in October 1983 this type of defect reached about 60 percent in the loaded new modules, the incidents of static discharge damage were recognized as being unusually frequent.

Corrective action for static discharge problems not only affects the costs of the products but also affects reliability and stabilized quality assurance; we traced the causes of electrostatic discharge in the card assembly process and reexamined the corrective actions.

### Objectives to Be Achieved and Target Completion Date

1. Current value — 59 percent of all defective modules are due to ESD.
2. Target value — one fifth of current value.
3. Activity deadline — end of September (with the verification of results to be done at the end of December).

### Promotion Organization and Activity Plan

See Figures 15-2 and 15-3.

### Understanding Current Circumstances

*Module failure analysis.* Of all module defects detected in the card test process, 59 percent are from damage caused by electrostatic discharge. (See Figure 15-4)

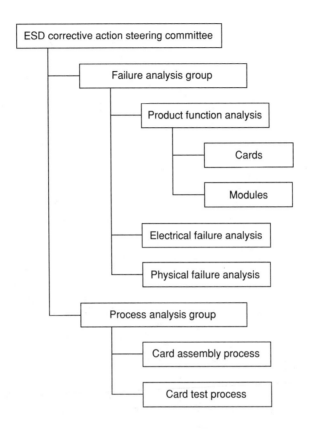

**Figure 15-2.  Promotion Organization for the ESD
Corrective Action**

| Action Items | Department | 1984 | | | | | | | | |
|---|---|---|---|---|---|---|---|---|---|---|
| | | A | M | J | J | A | S | O | N | D |
| Compilation of failure analysis data | Reliability Assurance Department | | | | | | | | | |
| Cause-and-effect analysis in all processes | Electrical Component Engineering Department | | | | | | | | | |
| Experiments to measure ESD | Electrical Component Engineering Department | | | | | | | | | |
| Process analysis | Reliability Assurance Department | | | | | | | | | |
| Improvement proposals | All departments | | | | | | | | | |
| Research | All departments | | | | | | | | | |
| Implementation of corrective actions | Applicable department | (first-aid measures) | | | | | | | | |
| Verification of the results | All departments | | | | | | | | | |

**Figure 15-3.  ESD Corrective Action Promotion Plan**

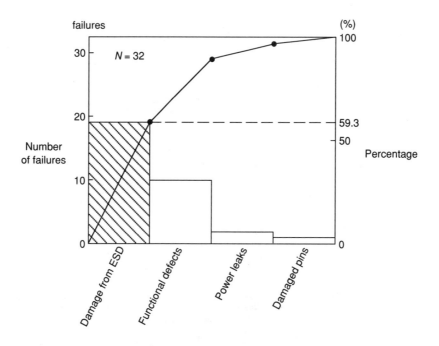

**Figure 15-4.  Failure Analysis Pareto Chart**

*Module ESD durability study.* With the parameters of 150 PF and 1.5kΩ, breakdowns in the modules begin at 500 V. When the modules are loaded on the cards, the breakdown levels are doubled. Also, the failure modes of the modules detected in the card test are the same as the failure modes of modules deliberately subjected to electrostatic discharge. (See Figure 15-5.)

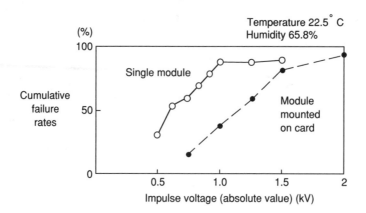

**Figure 15-5.  Distribution of Resistance to ESD**

*Analysis of causes in all processes.* See Figure 15- 6.

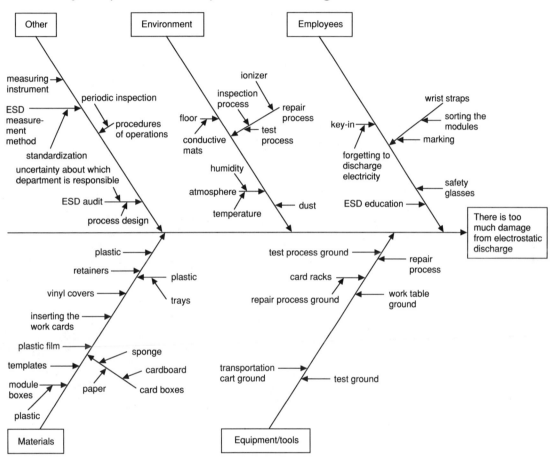

**Figure 15-6. Cause-and-effect Diagram of Electrostatic Discharge Damage**

## Measurements of and Experiments Involving Electrostatic Discharge

*Measurement of electric charge in the materials used.* See Figures 15-7 and 15-8.

*Cause-and-effect experiments involving the generation of static electrical charge in various processes.* We made cause-and-effect analyses of various processes using the design of experiments methods to investigate the interactions of various factors in the operating environment in generating static charge. (See Figure 15-9.)

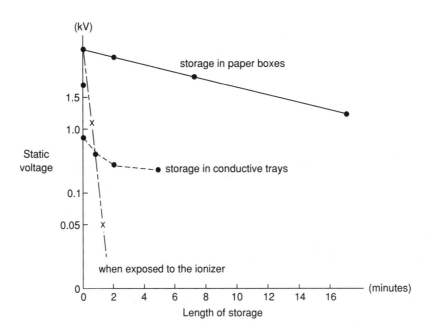

**Figure 15-7.  Electrostatic Discharge in the Sponge**

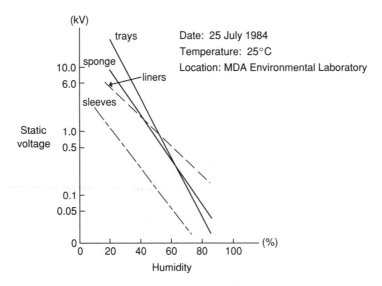

**Figure 15-8.  Humidity and Static Voltage in Working Materials**

| Stage | Purpose of Experiment | Detail of Experiment | | | Experimental Design | Notes |
|---|---|---|---|---|---|---|
| | | Generation of charge | Discharge | Conditions | | |
| 1. | • Preliminary experiment<br>• Standardization of measurement procedures | 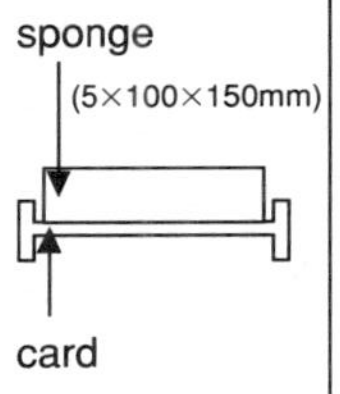 sponge<br>(5×100×150mm)<br>card | 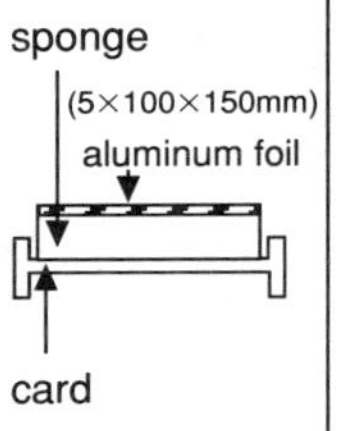 sponge<br>(5×100×150mm)<br>aluminum foil<br>card | Different people brush card 20 times with their hands | 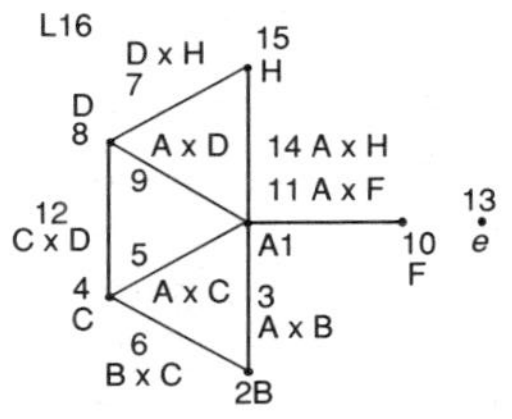 L16<br>D×H 15 H<br>D 7 A×D 14 A×H<br>8 9 11 A×F<br>12 C×D 5 A1 10 F<br>4 A×C 3 13 • e<br>C 6 A×B<br>B×C 2 B<br><br>A: human friction    D: tray<br>B: wrist strap    F: ionizer<br>C: work table    H: safety glasses | • The effects of the ionizer are great<br>• The wrist straps/trays are also significant<br>• There is little difference between people |
| 2. | • Cause factors — we eliminated people/ionizers and added floor mats to the experiment<br>• We did research in various processes | 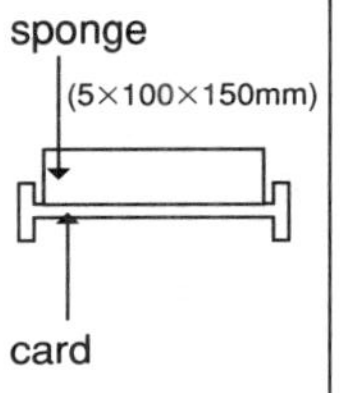 sponge<br>(5×100×150mm)<br>card | 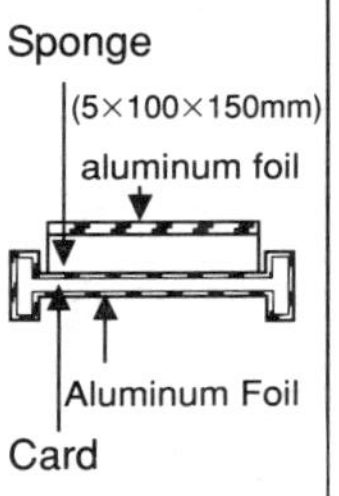 Sponge<br>(5×100×150mm)<br>aluminum foil<br>Aluminum Foil<br>Card | The same person brushes the card 20 times with a brush | 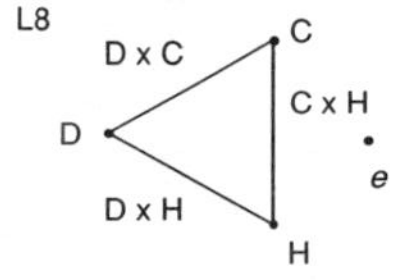 L8<br>C<br>D×C C×H<br>• e<br>D D×H H<br><br>D: floor mat<br>C: work table (with wrist strap)<br>H: safety glasses | • The floor mats also had great effects<br>• The static voltages generated were different in different locations, and were high in the mounting process |

**Figure 15-9. Cause-and-effect Experiments About the Generation of Static Electricity in Various Processes**

*Results of the experiments.*

1. The static charge in each of the materials used was correlated with the humidity — there is a danger to the modules when the materials are used in less than 50 percent humidity.
2. Countermeasures using ionizers and grounding are effective in discharging accumulated charge in the materials being used.
3. There are differences according to the operating environments of the various processes, with the major cause factors being ionizers and people. Also, we made interval estimations (within 95 percent confidence limits) from the results of a two-level experiment of various processes with and without antistatic measures. The results, presented in Figure 15-10, show that there is a large difference between having and not having the antistatic measures, and that there are large differences in the effectiveness of these measures between processes.

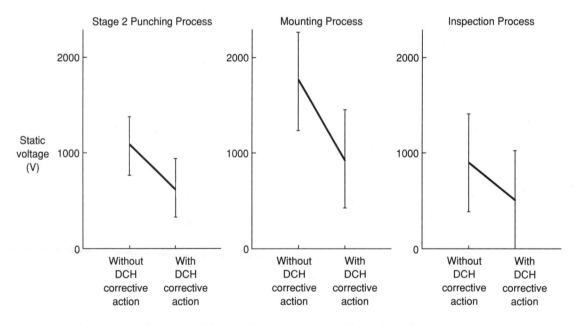

**Figure 15-10. Estimated Values of Static Charge Generated in Various Processes**

## Process Analysis

We made cause-and-effect matrices for the processes based on the results of the experiments and on measurements of generated static charges in each process, the grounding strategies, the parameters of the operations, the operating environments, and so forth. We used the matrices to perform an evaluation of the effects of the corrective action. (See Figure 15-11, page 126.)

### The Corrective Action Plan and Implementation

We established a corrective action plan on the basis of the above analysis, along with the circumstances for its execution. (See Table 15-1.)

### Checking Results

The changes in the module defect rates at the test process are shown in Figure 15-12.

### Topics for the Future

Through this project we learned the importance of establishing evaluations for the electrostatic discharges that arise in various processes, and the need for integrated ESD countermeasures that include all processes. In the future we will make an ESD audit system that includes continued verifications through evaluations that use the cause-and-effect matrices in each of the processes (Figure 15-11), standardization of process improvements, and standardization in the design of new processes.

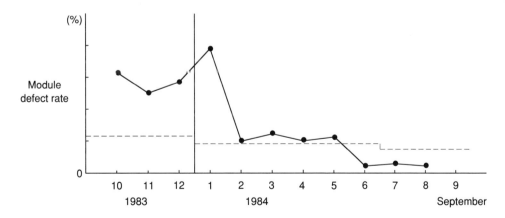

Figure 15-12. Improvement in Module Defect Rates in the Test Process

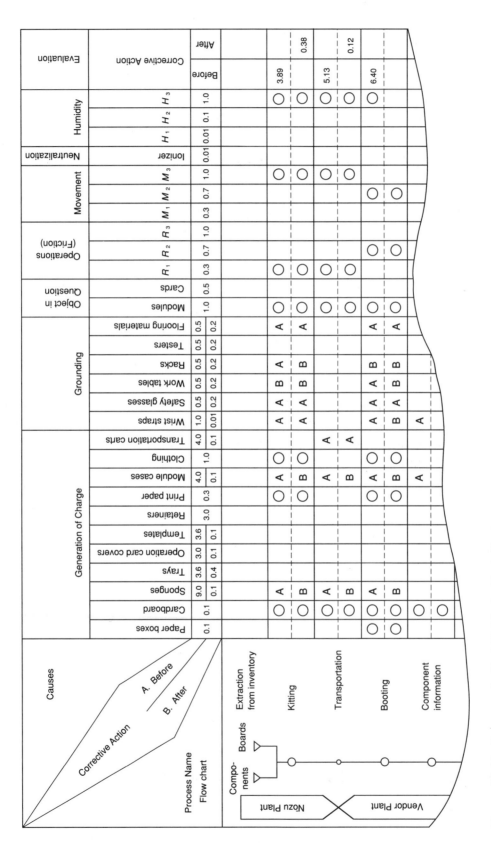

**Figure 15-11. Cause-and-effect Matrix for Each Process**

**Table 15-1. Execution of the Corrective Actions**

| Corrective Action Item | First-Aid Measures | | Corrective Actions | |
|---|---|---|---|---|
| | Detail of the Measures | Date Executed | Detail | Date Executed |
| ESD education on factory floor | Education about the importance of corrective actions for static electricity | February/March | Study performed on a periodic basis | Creation of an implementation overview by the last day of September |
| Improving the memory module linkage test | Improving the linkage test | February | Movement towards a periodic inspection system | Creation of an implementation overview by the last day of September |
| Modification of the module packing sponge | — | — | Use of static resistance sponge | Beginning in February |
| Use of conductive floor mats in test process | — | — | Use of conductive mats in the areas around the memory testers | Beginning in February |
| Retainers | Use of ionizers during operations | Since February | Request the research center to perform materials study | We expect a report by the end of June |
| Placement of cards into vinyl posting sheets | Introduction of operational methods so that the products are not directly contacted | From June on | Conversion to antistatic materials | Order on 8/17/84, implementation in November |
| Conversion of materials in slide-style packages | — | — | Conversion to antistatic packages | Cut over to new packages on 4/1/85 |
| Conversion of template materials | Abolishing the use of templates | From June on | Conversion to antistatic materials | Cut over to new templates 10/12/84 |
| Conversion of materials for card packing sponges | Introduction of operational methods so that the products are not directly contacted | From April on | Conversion to antistatic materials | Cut over to new sponges 1/10/85 |
| Conversion of plastic trays | Introduction of operations using antistatic trays | From June on | Conversion to antistatic materials in all circumstances | Cut over to new trays 1/10/85 |
| Transportation cart antistatic measures | — | — | Execution of conductive mat grounding | Beginning 9/30/84 |
| ESD audits | — | — | Study of scheduled/organized execution | Creation of an implementation overview by end of September |

# 16

# Problem Solving in Process Industries

## IMPORTANT POINTS

Many of Japan's predominant industries are process industries — steel (typified by blast furnaces and rolling equipment), oil refining and petrochemical processing (typified by refining towers, polymer towers, and piping), foodstuffs, spinning and textile, paper making, chemical, rubber, glass, and ceramics, to name a few.

In process industries the production equipment is relatively large, the manufacturing parameters and manufacturing processes (including constitution of raw materials, reaction temperatures, times, pressures and so forth) are set in advance, and the manufacturing is primarily done by equipment, with the people only controlling the machinery. Today many companies run their operations in this way with operators performing only monitoring functions from a remote control room.

In such companies, the success or failure of quality and productivity are largely determined by how the production equipment is used and how the manufacturing parameters are determined. If the manufacturing parameters are observed, then products with stabilized qualities are produced in a steady stream. While defective products due to careless mistakes (such as are seen in the manufacturing industries) are rare in the process industries, an entire lot can become defective with a single problem, and some problems can lead to catastrophic accidents such as factory explosions.

Consequently, the manufacturing parameters of raw materials mixing, melting temperatures, pressures, and so forth, should be set only after the optimal process parameters have been determined through use of various statistical methods, careful consideration of economic factors, and an understanding of what parameters are within the equipment limitations.

## CENTRAL CONCEPTS IN THIS EXAMPLE

As an example of problem solving in the processing industries, we present the improvement theme described by Toshimi Kumazaki of the Engineering Department of the Belt Division of Mitsuboshi Belts in the presentation meeting of the independent research groups in the 66th JUSE QC Seminar and Basic Course (Osaka).

This theme deals with changing the composition of raw materials to adapt to the increases in the demanded qualities of the users, and is a useful example of improving mixing parameters by zeroing in on problem areas using cause-and-effect diagrams and design of experiments methods.

## THEME: IMPROVING THE ABRASION DURABILITY AND RESISTANCE TO STICKING OF V-RIBBED BELTS

### Reason for Selection of Theme

V-ribbed belts are used for power transmission in automobile engines. The cross-section of the V-ribbed belts is shown in Figure 16-1.

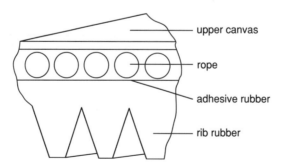

**Figure 16-1.   Structure of V-Ribbed Belts**

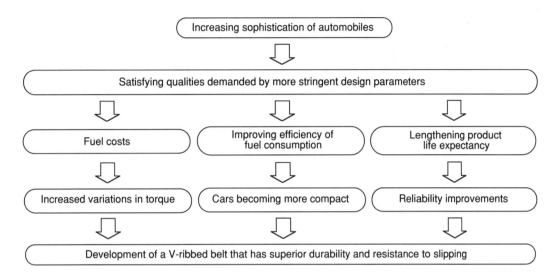

**Figure 16-2. Background of Stricter Demanded Qualities**

Each year the various automobile manufacturers make increasingly high-tech and high-quality automobiles; their demands for excellent V-ribbed belts with higher durability have become severe. (See Figure 16-2.)

However, when we improve the abrasion durability of the belt, we run into problems with sticking.

***The mechanism of sticking.*** Belt sticking arises during the early period of its use. Heat is generated in the belt, causing some of the rubber to become soft. The softened rubber collects in the grooves between ribs, causing the belts to stick. (See Figures 16-3 and 16-4.) Causes identified include:

- Causes related to the V-ribbed belts (rubber): Stress/strain characteristics, modulus of elasticity of 100 percent, hardness, and so on.
- Causes related to the pulleys: changes in torque, surface roughness and so on.

***The mechanism of abrasion.*** Because the power transmission mechanism of the V-ribbed belts is friction transmission, abrasion occurs from factors such as slip at the contact surface (shown in Figure 16-5) between the pulley and the belt.

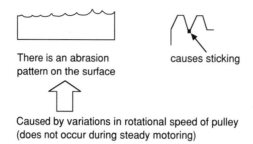

There is an abrasion
pattern on the surface

causes sticking

Caused by variations in rotational speed of pulley
(does not occur during steady motoring)

**Figure 16-3.   Magnified View of Belt Cross-section
After Use (Surface of Rubber)**

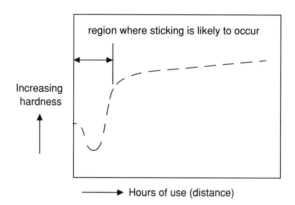

region where sticking is likely to occur

Increasing
hardness

→ Hours of use (distance)

**Figure 16-4.   General Pattern of Increasing Hardness of Rubber**

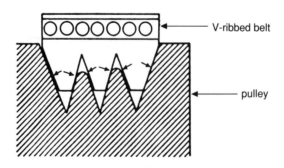

V-ribbed belt

pulley

**Figure 16-5.   Mechanism of Abrasion**

## Process Overview

V-ribbed belts are made through the mixing of raw rubber with vulcanizing agents, antioxidants, filling agents, and other ingredients. This step is followed by the rolling process, the fabrication process, and so forth. (See Figure 16-6.)

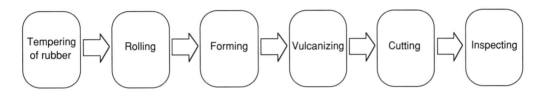

**Figure 16-6. Process Diagram**

## Establishment of Objectives

We were asked by auto manufacturer X, one of our largest consumers, to develop a V-ribbed belt that has greater resistance to abrasion and sticking than our current belts. We embarked on the development after establishing the following objectives:

1. General material characteristics of the rubber — no major changes from current characteristics (remaining within specified values)
2. Resistance to wear — wear rate in tests on actual machines of less than 0.9 percent
3. Resistance to sticking — no sticking in tests on actual machines

## Activity Plan

We adopted the theme in the second half of fiscal 1984 (November 1984 to March 1985) and formed a three member development team in the engineering department.

## Analysis of Causes

We used a cause-and-effect diagram to analyze the causes that have an influence on the wear and sticking of the belts. (See Figure 16-7.) Because the

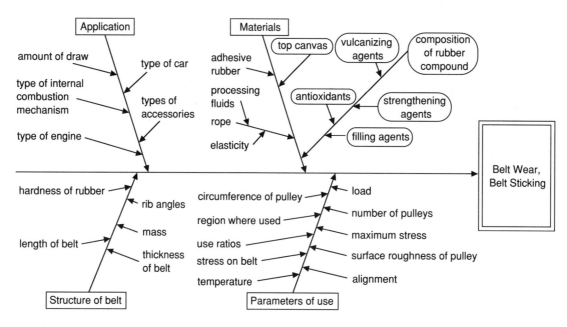

**Figure 16-7.  Cause-and-effect Diagram of Factors Influencing Belt Durability and Sticking**

parameters and conditions of belt use are dictated by the automobile manufacturers, and because we cannot change the structure of the belt, we decided to study the composition of the rubber.

As a first step, we addressed the selection of filling agent.

## Researching and Implementing Corrective Action Plans

***Selecting the filling agent.*** Because sticking is reduced when the rubber is compounded with filling agents, we performed preliminary tests using two sorts of filling agents (*P* and *Q*). We researched the results using these fillers.

    1. Composition (see Table 16-1)
    2. Results of quality evaluations
        a. Physical characteristics of rubber — There were no significant differences in the most important physical characteristics of the rubber (strength at the breaking point, coefficient of elongation at the breaking point, 100 percent modulus of elasticity, etc.) between the blank compound and the $P_1$, $P_2$, $Q_1$, and $Q_2$ compounds.

**Table 16-1.  Factors and Levels of Filling Agent Composition Test**

| Factor \ Level | None | $P_1$ | $P_2$ | $Q_1$ | $Q_2$ |
|---|---|---|---|---|---|
| Filling agent $P$ | 0 | 10 | 20 | —— | —— |
| Filling agent $Q$ | 0 | —— | —— | 10 | 20 |

Note:  Because combinations of filling agents $P$ and $Q$ cause adverse effects
on other characteristics, combinations of the two are not included in this test.

b. Tests on actual equipment using belts
  • Resistance to abrasion (see Figure 16-8).
  • Sticking — "Stickiness" is difficult to quantify; we evaluated the
    stickiness in this experiment in terms of "did stick" versus "didn't
    stick" (see Table 16-2).

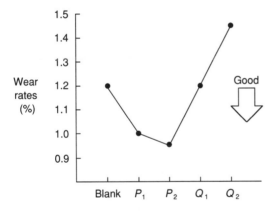

**Figure 16-8.  Durability**

**Table 16-2.  Evaluation of Sticking**

| Composition | Blank | $P_1$ | $P_2$ | $Q_1$ | $Q_2$ |
|---|---|---|---|---|---|
| Sticking | ✕ | ○ | ○ | ✕ | ✕ |

The result of this is that filling agent $P$ was verified as making beneficial
contributions in terms of both durability and sticking.

*Selecting the vulcanizing agent.* Because the rubber compounding agents
(that is, the vulcanizing agent $M$ and the antioxidant $T$, which we had been
using, and the filling agent $P$, which we had just selected) interact to influence

the physical properties of the rubber, we tested their combinations using a three-way layout method.

- We selected factors and levels (see Table 16-3).

**Table 16-3.   Factors and Levels in Combination Composition Test**

| Level | 1 | 2 |
|---|---|---|
| Vulcanizing agent $M$ | 3 | 6 |
| Filling agent $P$ | 10 | 20 |
| Antioxidant $T$ | 0.5 | 1 |

Note: Three-factor, two-level experiment — the trials for the eight combinations were run in a random order.

- We performed analysis of variance. For each experimental layout we looked at the physical properties of the rubber, performed analysis of variance, and studied the influence of each cause factor. For example:

  Stress/strain characteristics — analysis of variance of hardness (JIS-A) (see Table 16-4): When we pooled the interactions of $M \times P$, $M \times T$, and $P \times T$ with the error, the analysis of variance table shown in Table 16-5 was produced. We learned that the vulcanizing agent $M$ was significant to the 5 percent level. We performed analysis of variance on the other physical characteristics, getting the results shown in Figure 16-9.

**Table 16-4.   Analysis of Variance Table**

| Factor | $S$ | ø | $V$ | $F_0$ |
|---|---|---|---|---|
| $M$ | 70.5 | 1 | 70.5 | 5.78* |
| $P$ | 8.4 | 1 | 8.4 | — |
| $T$ | 11.3 | 1 | 11.3 | — |
| $M \times P$ | 3.5 | 1 | 3.5 | — |
| $M \times T$ | 2.8 | 1 | 2.8 | — |
| $P \times T$ | 4.7 | 1 | 4.7 | — |
| $E$ | 12.2 | 1 | 12.2 | — |
| Total | 113.4 | 7 | | |

**Table 16-5.   Analysis of Variance Table After Pooling**

| Factor | $S$ | ø | $V$ | $F_0$ |
|---|---|---|---|---|
| $M$ | 70.5 | 1 | 70.5 | 12.2* |
| $P$ | 8.4 | 1 | 8.4 | 1.4 |
| $T$ | 11.3 | 1 | 11.3 | 1.9 |
| $E$ | 23.2 | 4 | 5.8 | |
| Total | 113.4 | 7 | | |

| Factor | Vulcanizing Agent M | | Filling Agent P | | Antioxidant T | |
|---|---|---|---|---|---|---|
| Various material qualities | $M_1$ (3 parts) | $M_2$ (6 parts) | $P_1$ (10 parts) | $P_2$ (20 parts) | $T_1$ (0.5 parts) | $T_2$ (1 part) |
| Tension Characteristics — Hardness — JIS-A | 74.00* | 76.25 | 75.25 | 75.00 | 74.50 | 75.75 |
| Tension Characteristics — 100% modulus of elasticity | 6.50* | 8.43 | 7.53 | 7.40 | 7.25 | 7.68 |
| Tension Characteristics — Tension at breaking point (T.B.) | 14.30** | 17.13 | 15.98 | 15.45 | 15.75 | 15.68 |
| Tension Characteristics — Elongation at breaking point (E.B.) | 148.25* | 92.25 | 126.25 | 114.25 | 124.35 | |
| Tearing strength JIS-A | 64.50 | 62.75 | | | | |

NOTE:  * = Significant to 5%     ** = Significant to 1%

**Figure 16-9.  Summary of Results of Experiments**

- We performed belt use tests on actual equipment to evaluate the wear rates and sticking of the various rubbers. (See Figure 16-10.) None of the compounds had problems with sticking. The analysis of variance for wear rates is shown in Table 16-6.

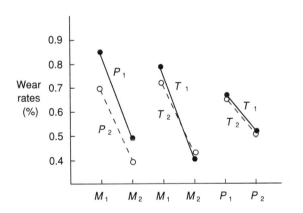

**Figure 16-10.  Wear Rates and Evaluations of Sticking**

**Table 16-6.  Analysis of Variance**

| Factor | S | ø | V | $F_0$ |
|---|---|---|---|---|
| M | 22.45 | 1 | 22.45 | 748.2** |
| P | 3.92 | 1 | 3.92 | 130.7** |
| T | 0.02 | 1 | 0.02 | 0.67 |
| M × T | 0.18 | 1 | 0.18 | 6.0 |
| E | 0.09 | 3 | 0.03 | |
| Total | 26.66 | 7 | | |

## Results

*Integrated evaluation.* Combining vulcanizing agent $M$, filling agent $P$, and antioxidant $T$, we found that in all of the eight experiments the wear rates were less than the targeted 0.9 percent and that there was no noticeable sticking.

At this point we carefully considered the various physical properties of the rubber, the wear, and the stickiness, along with the economic aspects, and concluded that $M_2$, $P_2$, $T_1$, are the optimal compounding parameters. We then ran a mass production test.

*Results of the mass production test.* We performed a mass production test compounding at $M_2$-$P_2$-$T_1$, using a company evaluation of the results and having automobile manufacturer $X$ perform an evaluation. Because these evaluations showed that the new compound is better than the old compound, we resolved to use this compound in our mass production from that time on.

## Topics for the Future

The objective of this theme activity was to develop a high-quality V-ribbed belt, and we achieved almost all of our initial goals. We want to use the experience we gained through this activity to assertively apply statistical methods such as design of experiment methods to new development themes.

# 17

# Problem Solving in
# the Construction Industry

## IMPORTANT POINTS

In the construction industry, as in any other field of production, arguments often arise that "even when we implemented TQC, there were no results," or that "TQC and the construction industry don't mix." In the construction industry these complaints are due mostly to certain characteristics that are peculiar to construction.

When compared with general manufacturing industries, the construction industry has some unique characteristics with respect to QC, giving rise to the following problems:

1. The construction industry is a build-to-order contract industry: The qualities of the product do not determine the orders.
2. It involves the manufacture of individual products: When there are particularly good results, standardization and horizontal diffusion is not possible because of changing parameters.
3. It is a migrant industry: When a construction project is completed, the QC circles and groups are completely dissolved.
4. The designers and the builders are different parties: There is no feedback from the builders to the designers, and there is a dearth of upstream prevention of problems.
5. It is an outdoor industry: The costs and the lead times are controlled by the weather.
6. It is an industry with multiple layers of subcontractors: "Quality" is built in by the subcontractors, so quality assurance is difficult.

7.  It is a labor-intensive industry: There are large numbers of different workers for each type of job, so adequate education is difficult.

Most of these problems either stem from misunderstandings and inadequate knowledge about TQC or are merely excuses for not using QC. Consequently, a company that is able to solve these problems can become dominant in the industry.

If TQC is dismissed as "not being part of the job," then problem solving is having problem awareness, discovering many problem areas, and solving problems through work system activities or group activities, which include QC philosophy. The procedures for problem solving in the construction industry are no different from those in any other industry.

Consider the following areas while solving problems:

1.  Having problem awareness while solving problems.
2.  Defining characteristics that show how bad the problems are.
3.  Accurately understanding facts through data.
4.  Sufficiently observing and understanding actual conditions.
5.  Correctly using QC methods and performing analysis to find the true causes.
6.  Combining the wisdom of all, synergistically merging creativity and innovation.
7.  Gaining approval from supervisors and cooperation from other departments, and running systematic, planned activities.

## CENTRAL CONCEPTS IN THIS EXAMPLE

As an example of problem solving in the construction industry we present the theme, "Ensuring the adhesion of exterior wall tiles in remodeling work," which was addressed by the Tokyo Branch of Maeda Construction Industries.

In this example, tests were performed in advance to discover the optimal parameters in all of the processes dealing with the tile, from the removal of the old blown-on wall covering to installation of the new exterior tile, to prevent new tiles from peeling off the superstructure of the building. These experiments resulted in great improvements in both quality and cost.

The evaluation of quality is difficult because the life cycle of construction products is so long. On the other hand, when there are claims, they usually have far-reaching effects that cause both the makers and the users great loss. Consequently, it is crucial that problems somehow be prevented before they occur rather than handled when they arise. The following is a good example of the development of an activity along these lines.

Also, when performing cause-and-effect analysis, the group in this example clearly defined its objectives, repeated experiments many times, and used analysis of experiments in defining optimal parameters based on facts and data.

This is a good example of customer orientation in problem solving to perform quality assurance — we hope that readers learn many valuable points from this case.

## THEME: ENSURING THE ADHESION OF EXTERIOR WALL TILES IN REMODELING WORK

### Overview of the Construction Project

*Name of project:* Remodeling of the *N* Assembly Hall

*Structure/scope:* Steel reinforced concrete construction, 5 levels below the ground, 5 levels above

*Application:* A meeting and reception hall

*Construction period:* 2/18/1985 through 9/30/85

*Floor space:* 15,200 $m^2$

*Area of blown-on products to be removed:* 1,680 $m^2$

*Area of porcelain tile:* 2,230 $m^2$

*Dimensions of porcelain tile:* 60 mm $\times$ 227 mm $\times$ 15 mm (two-leaf tiles)

*Time period for theme activities:* March to July, 1985

### Reason for Selection of Theme

This construction project is a remodeling of a building originally constructed by our company. Both the inside and the outside of the building are being remodeled to prepare it for a change in use. One of the points to which special attention must be paid is the removal of the 5-year-old exterior blown-on epoxy wall covering and its replacement with porcelain two-leaf tile. Our company has had no experience with large projects removing blown-on epoxy wall coverings, but we projected that the work methods used would have a large impact on schedules and costs. We also have to pay adequate attention to environmental issues such as noise and vibration, and consider measures for the safety of third parties.

After the building is completed, there must be absolutely no chance that the tiles will peel off. It is conceivable that the management of the removal of the blown-on epoxy wall covering will have a large influence on the quality of the tiling of the outer wall. However, because there are still many yet-to-be-defined quality assurance items and control standards in the process (which range from removing blown-on epoxy wall covering to installing exterior wall tile), we selected the above theme. Before entering the actual execution stage, we performed various experiments, clarified control points, and determined work methods so that we could be fully in control during execution of the project.

## Understanding Current Circumstances

*Detail of the construction processes to improve the exterior walls.* See Figure 17-1.

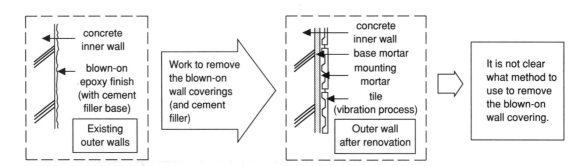

**Figure 17-1.  Summary Diagram of Renovation of External Walls**

*Profile irregularities of existing wall coverings.* See Figure 17-2.

*Forecasts of operational processes and causes of peeling tiles on outer walls.* We performed a study of the factors that cause tiles to peel, creating Figure 17-3.

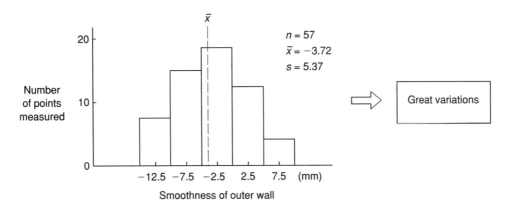

**Figure 17-2. Histogram of the Surface Irregularities of the External Walls**

## Analysis of Causes

***Study of blown-on covering removal rates.*** Although several methods of removing the blown-on wall coverings can be considered, the percentage of wall covering removed differs according to the process employed. Before selecting a process for the removal, we correlated the trade-offs between the percentage removal of the blown-on covering with the adhesive strength that the new tile will have on the outer walls; we then established control levels for the percentage of removal of the old wall covering.

*Experiment 1*

1. Purpose: To find the optimal percentage of blown-on wall covering removal by performing a one-dimensional experiment, the external wall tile adhesion strength as the output characteristic and a five-level input of the cause factor (the percentage of wall covering removed).
2. Conditions: We used in the experiment the tiles, base mortar, and mounting mortar that we were scheduled to use on the building. We used a vibration method for running the experiment, according to the standard operating procedures of our company.
   a. The method of the experiments: See Figure 17-4.
   b. The levels for the experiment:
      $A_1$ = No treatment to wall
      $A_2$ = Removal of only the protruding regions

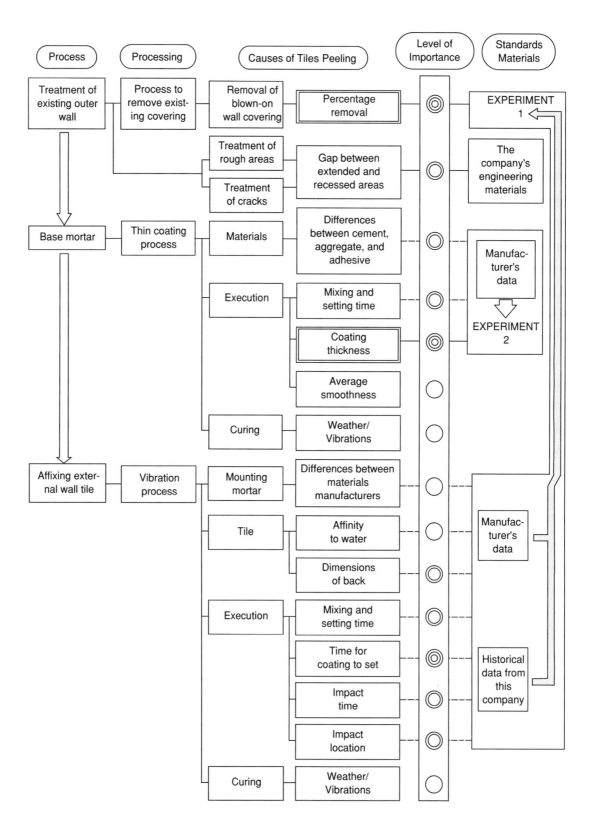

**Figure 17-3. Cause-and-effect Diagram of Peeling External Wall Tiles**

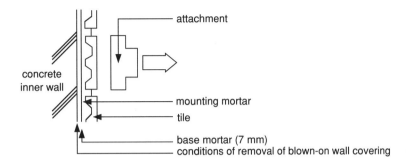

**Figure 17-4.  Overview of Experiment 1**

$A_3$ = 80 percent removal of the blown-on wall covering
$A_4$ = 90 percent removal of the blown-on wall covering
$A_5$ = 100 percent removal of the blown-on wall covering

c. Results of experiments: See Figure 17-5.

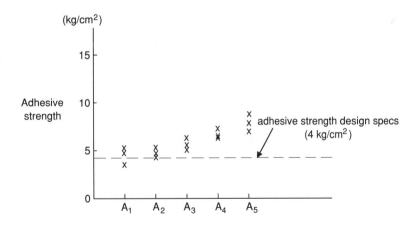

**Figure 17-5.  Results of Experiment 1**

d. Analysis of variance: See Table 17-1. Factor $A$ was significant to the 5
   percent level; we can say that the percentage of the blown-on wall
   covering has an effect on the adhesion strength of the outer tiles.
e. Confidence interval for the population average and for individual
   data: We calculated a 95 percent confidence interval for both the
   population average and the individual data. (See Figure 17-6.)

**Table 17-1. Analysis of Variable Table for Experiment 1**

| Factor | $S$ | $\phi$ | $V$ | $F_0$ | $F(0.05)$ |
|--------|-----|--------|-----|-------|-----------|
| $A$ | 20.23 | 4 | 5.06 | 12.97* | 3.48 |
| $E$ | 3.89 | 10 | 0.39 | | |
| $T$ | 24.12 | 14 | | | |

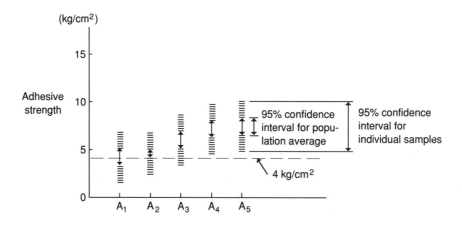

**Figure 17-6. Reliability Interval of Individual Data**

The result of these calculations was that we set the standard for the removal of the blown-on wall covering to level $A_2$ (90%).

   f. Determining the level of control: See Table 17-2.

**Table 17-2. Level of Control**

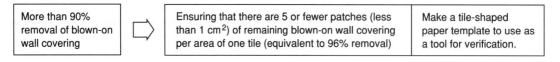

| More than 90% removal of blown-on wall covering | | Ensuring that there are 5 or fewer patches (less than 1 cm$^2$) of remaining blown-on wall covering per area of one tile (equivalent to 96% removal) | Make a tile-shaped paper template to use as a tool for verification. |

*Study of the method to remove the blown-on wall covering.*

*Experiment 2*

1. Purpose: To select a method for trial and compare it through experimentation to demanded abilities to determine which method to use.
2. Conditions: We selected 1 m$^2$ units on the wall of the site, and ran experimental methods on each.

3. Results of experiments: See Table 17-3. We tested four methods (stripping agents, sanders, etc.) of removing the blown-on wall covering, comparing the noise, dust, vibration, removal efficiency, removal percentage, degree of damage to the underlying wall, and cost. On the basis of these comparisons we decided to use the stripping agent method. However, because permeation of the stripping agent into the underlying cement filler was poor, we decided to research improvement plans.

**Research on ways to delay the hardening of the stripping agent for better permeation.** See Figure 17-7.

*Experiment 3*

1. Purpose: To implement corrective actions and then to verify the results in delaying the hardening of the stripping agent.
2. Experimental method and results: See Table 17-5. We adopted a method of seal curing the stripping agent into the wall, and researched the most appropriate time to let the stripping agent permeate the cement filler.

**Researching the most appropriate time to allow the stripping agent to permeate the cement filler.**

*Experiment 4*

1. Purpose: To observe the effects on the efficiency of the removal method. We ran a two-way layout experiment (without repetitions), with four levels for the polyethylene film cover and three levels of underlying cement filler surface ratios as experimental elements.
2. Conditions: After coating with a standard amount of the stripping agent (1 kg/m$^2$), we preserved the coating with a 0.3 mm polyethylene film, let it sit, and removed the blown-on coating with a chisel.

   The levels we used were as follows:

   $B_1$ = 15 percent of underlying cement filler
   $B_2$ = 55 percent of underlying cement filler
   $B_3$ = 100 percent of underlying cement filler
   $C_1$ = 1 hour sitting time
   $C_2$ = 2 hours sitting time
   $C_3$ = 3 hours sitting time
   $C_4$ = 4 hours sitting time

**Table 17-3. Comparisons of the Removal Processes**

| Item | Demanded Attributes | Removal Methods | | | | Level of Importance |
|---|---|---|---|---|---|---|
| | | Stripping Agent | Sander | Chipper | Sledge Hammer | |
| Noise | Must be less than 60 decibels at the property line | ◎ 55-60 decibels (background noise) | × 65-70 decibels | × 70-75 decibels | ○ 66-60 decibels | ◎ |
| Dust | Not producing any | ◎ None | × For the most part, entire coating becomes dust | △ Part of the coating becomes dust | △ Part of the coating becomes dust | ○ |
| Vibration | Being undetectable to humans | ◎ None | ◎ None | △ A bit | ○ A bit | ○ |
| Efficiency | 4.5 m²/worker/day | △ 2.6 m²/worker/day | △ 3.7 m²/worker/day | ○ 7.6 m²/worker/day | × 1.4 m²/worker/day | ○ |
| Under layers | Removal of 90% or more of the blown-on wall covering | ○ 90~100% | △ 80~100% | ◎ 95~100% | × 70~80% | ◎ |
| | Amount of damage to the inner wall | ○ No damage | △ Scrapes on inner wall surface 0-1 mm deep | × Pits in inner wall surface about 10 mm deep | △ Grooves in inner wall 1-2 mm deep | ◎ |
| Cost | Less than $_____ | △ $_____ | △ $_____ | ◎ $_____ | × $_____ | ○ |
| First-order decision (overall factors) | | ○ A problem with efficiency | △ Eliminated because of problems with noise and dust | × Eliminated because of problems with noise | × Eliminated because of problems with removal and efficiency | |

⟹ The method of treating with a stripping agent is the best plan. A study was done to improve its efficiency.

**Table 17-4.  Consideration of the Results of Experiment 2**

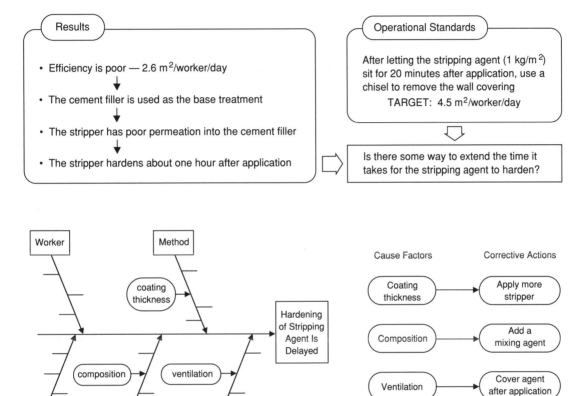

**Figure 17-7.  Cause-and-effect Diagram for Delaying the Hardening of the Stripper, and Corrective Action Plan**

**Table 17-5.  Detail and Results of Experiment 3**

| Method | Detail of Experiment | Results of Experiment | Conclusions |
|---|---|---|---|
| Applying more stripper | We applied 1.5 kg/m$^2$ and 2.0 kg/m$^2$ (a coating of more than 2.5 kg/m$^2$ is difficult) | Hardened in 60-90 minutes; permeation into cement filler was slight. | No effects |
| Adding a mixing agent | There is no appropriate mixing agent We mixed in a volatile solvent | Hardened in 40-60 minutes; reduced permeation of blown-on coating | " |
| Curing through sealing | We perfectly sealed the stripping agent with a polyethylene film | Hardened after 3 hours There is permeation of the cement liner | There are effects |

3. Results of experiments: See Figure 17-8.

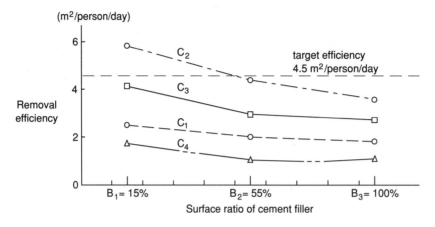

**Figure 17-8. Results of Experiment 4**

4. Analysis of variance table: See Table 17-6. Factors $B$ and $C$ were significant to the 5 percent level; we can say that the surface ratio of the cement filler and the time that the coating was allowed to sit both influence the efficiency of the removal process. As Figure 17-8 shows, $C_2$ has the most efficient removal.

**Table 17-6. Analysis of Variance Table for Experiment 4**

| Factor | S | $\phi$ | V | $F_0$ | F (0.05) |
|--------|------|----|------|-------|----------|
| B | 5.18 | 2 | 2.59 | 15.5* | 5.14 |
| C | 17.85 | 3 | 5.95 | 35.6* | 4.76 |
| E | 1.00 | 6 | 0.17 | | |
| Total | 24.03 | 11 | | | |

5. Estimates of the population average: When we make point estimations of the population averages of the combinations of elements $B$ and $C$, we get Table 17-7. Because we cannot artificially manipulate element $B$, we took an average of the values given using element $C_2$, that is to say, the average of $B_1C_2$, $B_2C_2$, and $B_3C_2$. The average value was 4.47 m² per worker per day. We initially predicted that using $C^2$ the removal efficiency would nearly fulfill the target of 4.5 m² per worker per day.

**Table 17-7. Estimations of Population Averages**

|         | $C_1$ | $C_2$ | $C_3$ | $C_4$ |
|---------|-------|-------|-------|-------|
| $B_1$   | 2.95  | 5.36  | 3.96  | 2.09  |
| $B_2$   | 1.84  | 4.28  | 2.88  | 1.01  |
| $B_3$   | 1.34  | 3.78  | 2.38  | 0.51  |

$\Downarrow$

4.47 m²/person/day

***Modifying the operational standards.*** As a result of our research, we modified the stripping agent operational standards as follows:

1. After coating with stripping agent (1 kg/m²), cover with 0.3 mm polyethylene film.
2. Let it sit for two hours.
3. Using a chisel, remove the blown-on wall coating with the base layer.

***Study of the thickness of the base mortar.*** From a histogram of the profile irregularities on the outer surface of the core wall, we think that the irregularities are mostly −15 to 7 mm. (See Figure 17-9.)

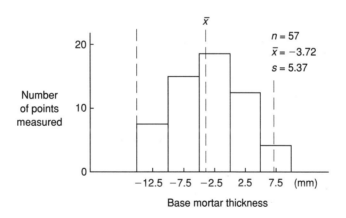

**Figure 17-9. Histogram of the Surface Irregularities of Existing Outer Wall**

From our experiments, we can verify the mortar adhesion strength when the base mortar is between 2 and 24 mm.

*Verifying the adhesion strength of the base mortar.*

*Experiment 5*

1.  Purpose: We selected five levels of coating thicknesses from the range of coating thicknesses in the base mortar (2 through 24 mm), and performed a one-dimensional experiment linking the thickness of the coating to the strength of adhesion.
2.  Conditions: We used the same base mortar in the experiment that we were scheduled to use in the construction, and performed the thin mortar coating as per operational standards.
    * Experimental method: See Figure 17-10.
    * Levels of thickness of the base mortar:
      $D_1$ = 2 mm
      $D_2$ = 7 mm
      $D_3$ = 12 mm
      $D_4$ = 18 mm
      $D_5$ = 24 mm

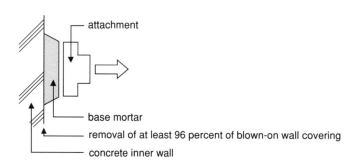

**Figure 17-10.  Overview of Experiment 5**

3.  Experimental results: See Figure 17-11.
4.  Analysis of variance: See Table 17-8.
5.  Results of analysis: Factor $D$ is *not* significant to the 5 percent level. Consequently, we cannot say that the differences in thickness of the base mortar exert an influence on the strength of adhesion. We can say that the strength of adhesion satisfies the design standards of 4 kg/cm$^2$.

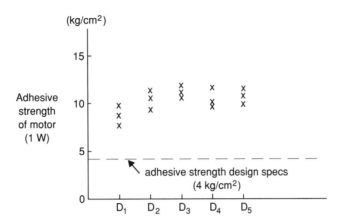

**Figure 17-11.  Results of Experiment 5**

**Table 17-8.  Analysis of Variance Table for Experiment 5**

| Factor | S | $\phi$ | V | $F_0$ | F (0.05) |
|--------|-------|-----|------|------|---------|
| C | 10.05 | 4 | 2.51 | 2.26 | 3.48 |
| E | 11.05 | 10 | 1.11 | | |
| T | 21.10 | 14 | | | |

## Implementation Plan

On the basis of the results of the experiments, we created a construction plan, expressed in the QC process chart and operational standards. (See Figure 17-12.)

## Results of Implementation

1. Figure 17-13 shows the tile adhesion strength that resulted from construction performed on the basis of this plan. The variability was small, the strength of adherence was assured, and the finish of the tiles had only very small surface irregularities.

QC Process Chart  (Excerpts)

| Unit Processes | Control Characteristics | Control Levels | Procedures | Timing | Frequency | Standards Diagrams | Management | Actions |
|---|---|---|---|---|---|---|---|---|
| Removal of the blown-on wall covering | Amount of remaining blown-on wall covering | 5 patches or less (1cm² or smaller) remaining per tile-sized area | Using a board for checking | When the operations are complete | Once a day | Experiment 1 | A graph of the number of reworks | Re-removal |
| Base mortar layer | Mortar thickness | 2-24 mm | Using a bob | After wall covering removed | Every span | Experiment 2 | Check sheets | Chipping, etc. |

Operational Standards  (Excerpts)

| Unit Operations | Detail of the Operation | | Cautions |
|---|---|---|---|
| Applying the stripping agent | Amount of stripping agent:  1 kg/m² | | The size of the film is 0.9m × 0.6 m. |
| | After coating seal with surface for 2 hours with polyethylene film | | Record time data on the film when using it. |

**Figure 17-12.  The Operational Standards in the QC Process Chart**

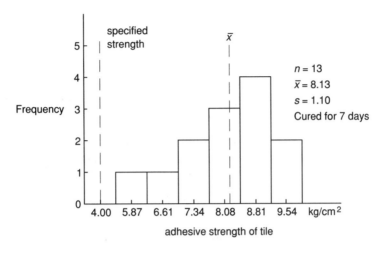

**Figure 17-13.  Results of Tests Pulling on the Tiles**

2.  Figure 17-14 shows the effects of the improved method of removing the blown-on wall covering in terms of cost and removal efficiency. Although the cost reductions and removal efficiencies were slightly less than expected (because of the influence of the base cement filler ratios), we were satisfied with the results.

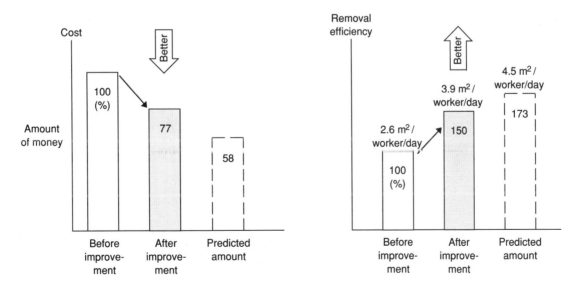

**Figure 17-14.  Results of Improvements to the Removal Process**

**Problem Areas and Review**

1. We think that the differences between projected and actual costs and efficiencies in the blown-on wall coating removal process were due to our lack of knowledge about the base cement filler (its surface area, for example). To predict more accurately, we must thoroughly research the actual circumstances so we can feed the data back into the implementation plan, effectively use QC methods, and perform experiments.
2. Although it was possible to compare the various methods of removal through small scale experiments, some items could not be compared within the requirement levels. It was necessary to research even more effective experimental methods.

# 18

# Problem Solving
# in Service Industries

## IMPORTANT POINTS

TQC has come to be enthusiastically used in the service industries. When you speak of TQC in the service industries, you are speaking of a TQC no different from the TQC that was developed in the manufacturing industries. Although the philosophy is the same, we still need to know how to approach the qualities chosen as the targets of TQC activities; we must define what the "qualities of service" are in order to perform analysis of quality service. Table 18-1 presents examples of quality in the service industries.

To raise the levels of these qualities — in other words, to perfect the service activities that will earn customer satisfaction — it is important to continuously perform the management cycle of plan, do, check, action (PDCA), ensuring continuity from the source of the activities to the last process.

There are three categories of qualities in the service industry:

1. *Qualities that can be expressed quantitatively:* These include qualities such as portion sizes in restaurants, room size and bed comfort levels in hotels, accuracy of train and airline schedules, accuracy of the receipts in supermarkets, and waiting times at supermarket checkout counters or at taxi stands.

2. *Qualities that are expressed in terms of the user's subjective response rather than in terms of objective values of characteristics:* Such qualities are apparent in the greetings of waiters and taxi drivers, in directional signs on expressways, and in the impression you get when you take your seat in a train or an airplane, for example.

3. *Qualities that are necessary to ensure safety and reliability:* Maintenance of airplanes, trains, and buses, and equipping of hotels with fire safety

157

### Table 18-1.  Quality in the Service Industries

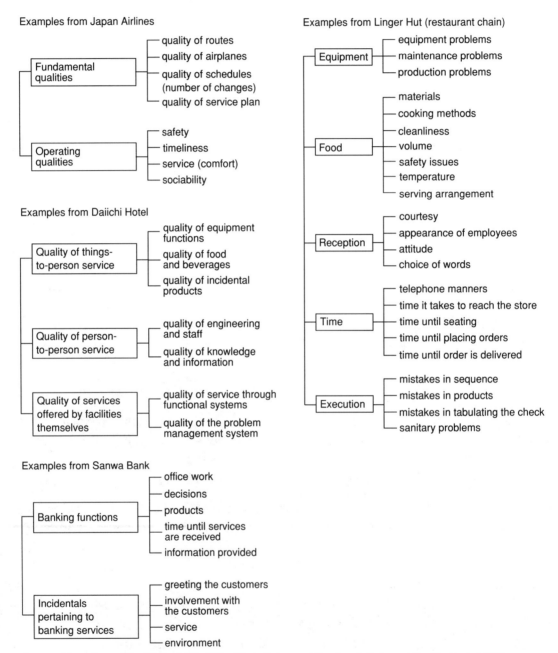

Examples from Japan Airlines

Fundamental qualities
— quality of routes
— quality of airplanes
— quality of schedules (number of changes)
— quality of service plan

Operating qualities
— safety
— timeliness
— service (comfort)
— sociability

Examples from Daiichi Hotel

Quality of things-to-person service
— quality of equipment functions
— quality of food and beverages
— quality of incidental products

Quality of person-to-person service
— quality of engineering and staff
— quality of knowledge and information

Quality of services offered by facilities themselves
— quality of service through functional systems
— quality of the problem management system

Examples from Sanwa Bank

Banking functions
— office work
— decisions
— products
— time until services are received
— information provided

Incidentals pertaining to banking services
— greeting the customers
— involvement with the customers
— service
— environment

Examples from Linger Hut (restaurant chain)

Equipment
— equipment problems
— maintenance problems
— production problems

Food
— materials
— cooking methods
— cleanliness
— volume
— safety issues
— temperature
— serving arrangement

Reception
— courtesy
— appearance of employees
— attitude
— choice of words

Time
— telephone manners
— time it takes to reach the store
— time until seating
— time until placing orders
— time until order is delivered

Execution
— mistakes in sequence
— mistakes in products
— mistakes in tabulating the check
— sanitary problems

Source:  Kozo Koura, "Quality Control in Office Work, Sales, and Service, 3, Universal Quality Control (2)," *Standardization and Quality Control*, 37 (11):  43-52, 1984.

systems fall into this category. This is an indirect quality, as compared with the first two types, which are direct qualities.

To solve problems in a service industry it is important to clearly define the qualities of the service, to define the corresponding levels of characteristics, and to identify root causes by collecting data and performing analyses. Furthermore, although quality assurance and standardization systems are not yet generally found in the service industries, these too need to be realized.

## CENTRAL CONCEPTS IN THIS EXAMPLE

We take for an example the maintenance of kitchen equipment in the Linger Hut, a company in the food service industry.[1] Linger Hut has a chain of 93 direct sales noodle shops — Nagasaki Chanpon Noodles and Nagasaki Saraudon Noodle — across the country. In any food service enterprise, quality types 1 (seasoning of the food, placement on the dishes, size of portions, etc.), 2 (manners and behavior of the waiters and cooks, etc.), and 3 (proper functioning of equipment) are equally important.

This company achieved great success by performing the steps of understanding actual circumstances, analyzing causes, devising corrective actions, evaluating the actions, and executing them, performing each step of standardization, and creating a management system to simplify maintenance activities in each store.

## THEME: CREATING A MAINTENANCE SYSTEM FOR EQUIPMENT AND MACHINERY

### Reason for Selection of Theme

*Fundamental maintenance philosophy.* "Providing good food, with good feelings, in a comfortable environment." The functioning of the equipment and machinery has the greatest influence on this fundamental mission statement. If

---

[1] Hiroki Nakano, "Creating a Maintenance System for Equipment and Machinery," *Quality Control*, 36:192-97, 1985.

the equipment and machinery is functioning correctly, then it is possible, to some degree, to bring satisfaction to the customers. To ensure its proper functioning, the following requirements must be satisfied.

- Maintenance must be able to be performed simply in the shops.
- There must be a defined daily management system.
- There must be a defined periodic inspection system.
- There must be a defined system of feedback about the design of the stores.

The fundamental philosophy of maintenance is prevention.

Aligning with higher-level policies and direction. After receiving the sales division direction to "maintain last year's customer counts in existing stores" and the Kyūshū administrative region's action item, "improve the maintenance system," the maintenance manager decided to pretest a maintenance system in district 2 of the North Region.

## Understanding Current Circumstances

First, survey the existing maintenance system. A survey of the existing maintenance system in the Kyūshū sales district revealed that the system would be inadequate to future requirements and needed to be improved. (See Figure 18-1.)

Second, survey the problems with equipment and machines. Using a checklist, we ran a study of the condition of the equipment in the North Region District 2 between June 20 and June 27, 1984. Based on the results, we made Pareto charts of the problems with the equipment and machinery and with the kitchen equipment.

The Pareto charts indicated that there were many problems with the kitchen equipment (equipment primarily used for cooking), and that problems with the dumpling makers, noodle boilers, and soup warmers were especially prevalent. These are the primary implements used in making our main products; if they function improperly we cannot provide the customers with products that satisfy them, nor can we hope make progress in energy conservation.

To combat this state of affairs we needed to establish both a daily periodic inspection system and a maintenance management system. (See Figure 18-2.)

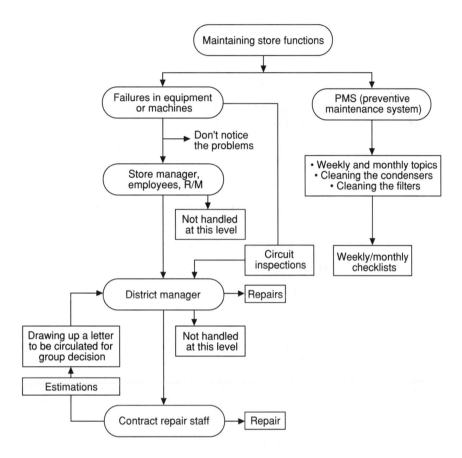

**Figure 18-1. Current Maintenance Flow Chart**

Third, investigate the cost of repairs. We analyzed the repair expenses in the North Region District 2, beginning with the December 1983 expenses. In December, January, and February, the district had tripled its repair budget because of unexpected and accumulated problems. Although the district remained within its budget in March, April, May, and June, the needs for repairs were accumulating, as was seen in the second step of understanding actual circumstances.

As a result of our investigations, we concluded that it was necessary to control the repair items within budgets, and to understand the particulars and the costs of each repair. It was also necessary to reduce costs by performing the repairs internally.

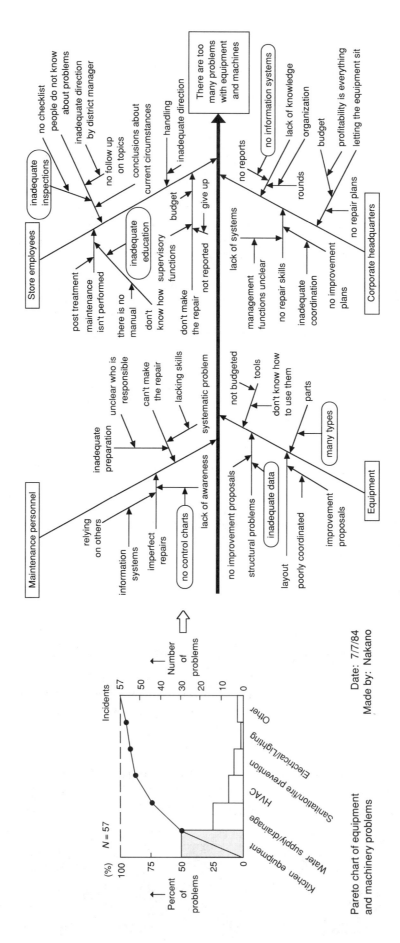

Cause-and-effect diagram for equipment and machinery problems

Pareto chart of equipment and machinery problems

Date: 7/7/84
Made by: Nakano

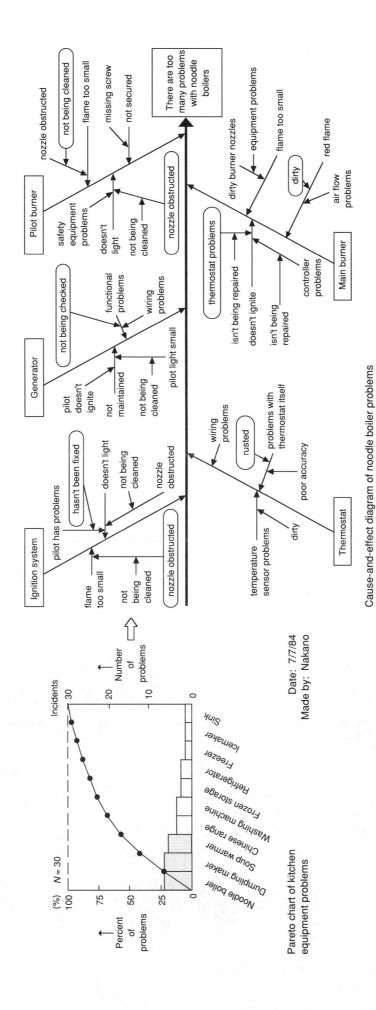

Cause-and-effect diagram of noodle boiler problems

Pareto chart of kitchen
equipment problems

Date: 7/7/84
Made by: Nakano

**Figure 18-2. Audit of Equipment and Machinery Problem Areas**

## Analysis of Causes

According to the Pareto chart of problems with equipment and machinery, the kitchen equipment accounts for about 50 percent of all of the problems. We surveyed the store managers in the North Region District 2 to determined their knowledge of kitchen equipment. We also analyzed their knowledge of maintenance issues.

Figure 18-3 shows the results of a questionnaire given to the six store managers in the North Region District 2. The results indicate that an overwhelming percentage of the store managers — those who run the stores — have never repaired store equipment or don't know how to repair it. We decided that lack of education was a definite problem.

Looking at the major cause factors for the large number of broken equipment and machines (Figure 18-2) we can say that (1) the system for reporting equipment problems to corporate headquarters is inadequate, (2) there are not enough data on which to base decisions about the state of equipment and machines, (3) there are no checklists with which to verify repairs when problems occur, and (4) the company employees in the shops don't have sufficient knowledge.

We also studied the noodle boilers, which had the most problems of any type of kitchen equipment, and were able to identify the cause factors, shown in the boxes in Figure 18-2, that contribute to the effect characteristic "Too many broken noodle boilers."

## Corrective Actions

For each of the problem areas, we established demanded characteristics for the system. For each of these demanded characteristics we established substitute or counterpart characteristics that could be concretely addressed, thus making a preliminary design for the maintenance system.

Demanded characteristic 1:   Maintain machinery and equipment so that they operate properly.

Substitute characteristic 1:  Repair existing problems.

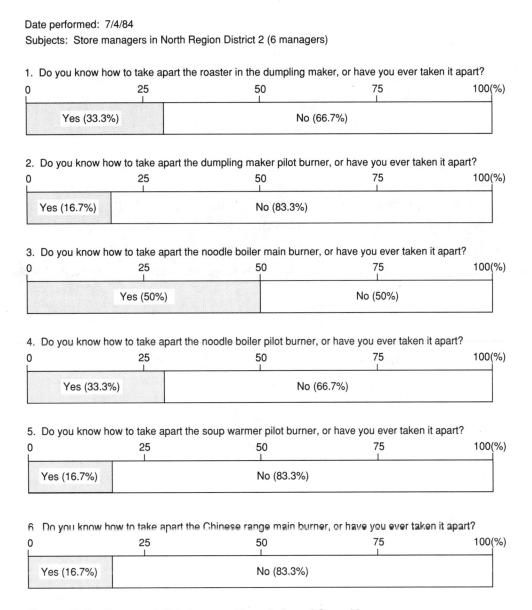

Date performed: 7/4/84

Subjects: Store managers in North Region District 2 (6 managers)

1. Do you know how to take apart the roaster in the dumpling maker, or have you ever taken it apart?

| 0 | 25 | 50 | 75 | 100(%) |

Yes (33.3%) — No (66.7%)

2. Do you know how to take apart the dumpling maker pilot burner, or have you ever taken it apart?

| 0 | 25 | 50 | 75 | 100(%) |

Yes (16.7%) — No (83.3%)

3. Do you know how to take apart the noodle boiler main burner, or have you ever taken it apart?

| 0 | 25 | 50 | 75 | 100(%) |

Yes (50%) — No (50%)

4. Do you know how to take apart the noodle boiler pilot burner, or have you ever taken it apart?

| 0 | 25 | 50 | 75 | 100(%) |

Yes (33.3%) — No (66.7%)

5. Do you know how to take apart the soup warmer pilot burner, or have you ever taken it apart?

| 0 | 25 | 50 | 75 | 100(%) |

Yes (16.7%) — No (83.3%)

6. Do you know how to take apart the Chinese range main burner, or have you ever taken it apart?

| 0 | 25 | 50 | 75 | 100(%) |

Yes (16.7%) — No (83.3%)

**Figure 18-3. Survey of Maintenance Knowledge of Store Managers**

Substitute characteristic  2:   Perform periodic inspections of stores.

Substitute characteristic 3:   Perform periodic maintenance in stores.

Demanded characteristic 2:    Perform statistical control pertaining to repairs.

Substitute characteristic:    Control the costs, content, and frequency of repairs.

Demanded characteristic 3:    Provide education about the equipment.

Substitute characteristic:    Perform Off-JT and OJT pertaining to the kitchen equipment.

Using the substitute characteristics to help fulfill the demanded characteristics, we ran a preliminary test of the maintenance system in the North Region District 2.

For demanded characteristic 1, we performed the following activities:

- We categorized the necessary repairs of current problems as "external repairs" or "internal repairs." The external repairs were handled by the maintenance manager, while the internal repairs were performed by the district manager and the maintenance manager.
- Using a checklist, the store managers performed weekly inspections and checks of the equipment and machines in the stores, and reported the results to the district managers.
- Corporate headquarters determined scheduled maintenance items and saw to it that store managers performed the maintenance on a monthly basis.

For demanded characteristic 2, we did the following:

- To control costs, content, and frequency of repairs, we made the repairs as a starting point, and then we input into personal computers data on costs and details of equipment failures as they happened.

For demanded characteristic 3, we performed the following activities:

- We performed Off-JT and OJT in kitchen equipment. For the Off-JT we used videotapes and manuals, and held regional leaders' meetings. We divided OJT between the maintenance manager and the district manager, who trained the store managers in repair procedures.

## Results

The activities yielded these results:

1. The results in terms of demanded characteristic 1 are shown in Figures 18-4 (a), (b), and (c). There is a great reduction in the number of problems: whereas before the corrective action there were 57 equipment problems at one time in the six shops in the district, there are now only 7. Although the current four-month average for the performance of periodic inspections is 79.6 percent (below our target of 90 percent), it has become easy for the district manager and the maintenance manager to gather data. The four-month average for the performance of periodic maintenance is 53.6 percent, (below our target of 70 percent); however, the number of failures of kitchen equipment has fallen.
2. The results in terms of demanded characteristic 2 are that currently there are continuing statistics available, and that monthly data on repair costs, details, and frequencies are understood. However, there is still the need to systematize the methods of obtaining data.
3. The results in terms of demanded characteristic 3 are shown in Figure 18-5. Whereas only one manager (of the six) had passable maintenance skills before the corrective action, now four have those skills. However, our goal of having all the managers qualified to perform maintenance has still not been achieved.

## Standardization

As a result of the pretest run in North Region District 2, we planned the Stage 2 maintenance system, shown in Figure 18-6.

## Review and Topics for the Future

Still needed after implementation of corrective action in North Region District 2 are the following actions:

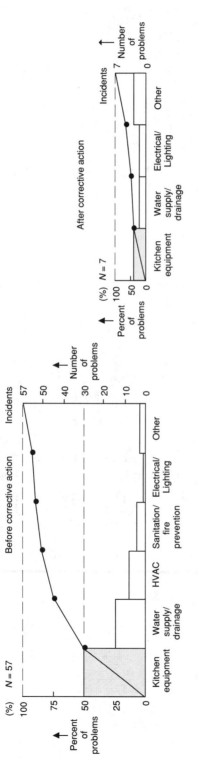

(a) Pareto chart of problems with equipment and machines

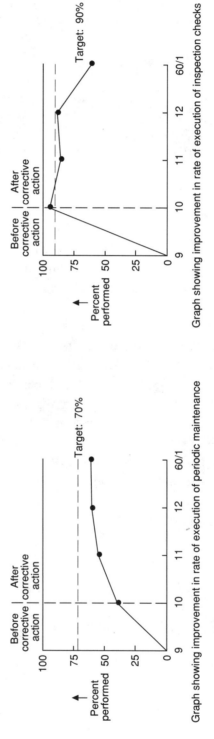

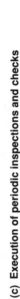

(c) Execution of periodic inspections and checks

(b) Execution of periodic maintenance

Figure 18-4.   The Results of the Corrective Action

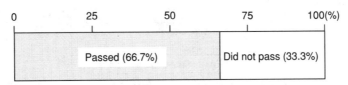

Subjects: North Region District 2 Store Managers (6 Managers)

**Figure 18-5.  Execution of Education about the Equipment**

1. Renovation of the equipment and machinery in existing stores.
2. Establishment of maintenance standards and education for district managers and store managers, as well as establishment of a follow-up to the education program.
3. Systematization of the procedures through which data are obtained, and reexamination of management materials for data collection.

It would be extremely difficult to resolve these problem areas immediately, and currently no preventive maintenance system is in place. In the future we would like to establish equipment management standards as well as district manager and store manager maintenance standards. We would like to perform education based on those standards, and to make a Ringer Hut preventive maintenance system based on pretests in the various district units.

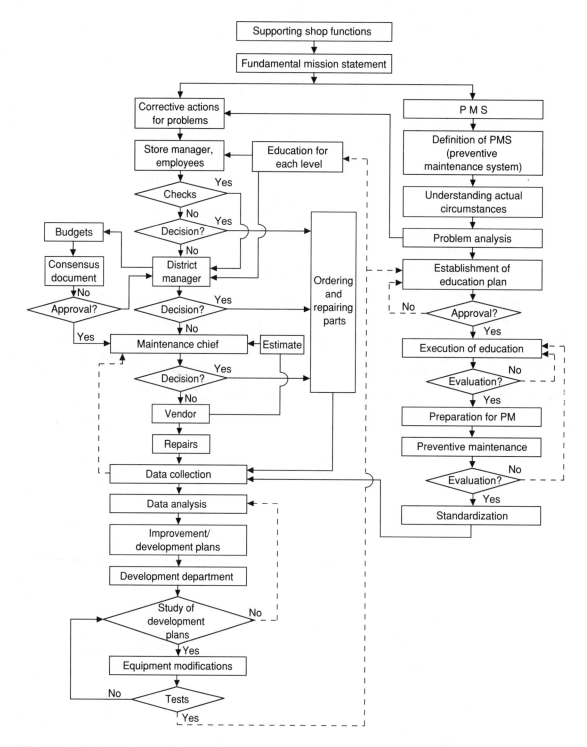

**Figure 18-6. Flow Chart of Stage 2 Maintenance System**

# Index

# Other Books on Quality

Productivity Press publishes and distributes materials on continuous improvement in productivity, quality, customer service, and the creative involvement of all employees. Many of our products are direct source materials from Japan that have been translated into English for the first time and are available exclusively from Productivity. Supplemental products and services include newsletters, conferences, seminars, in-house training and consulting, audio-visual training programs, and industrial study missions. Call 1-800-274-9911 for our free book catalog.

## Quality Function Deployment
### Integrating Customer Requirements into Product Design
*edited by Yoji Akao*

More and more, companies are using quality function deployment, or QFD, to identify their customers' requirements, translate them into quantified quality characteristics and then build them into their products and services. This casebook introduces the concept of quality deployment as it has been applied in a variety of industries in Japan. The materials include numerous case studies illustrating QFD applications. Written by the creator of QFD, this book provides direct source material on Quality Function Deployment, one of the essential tools for world class manufacturing. It is a design approach based on the idea that quality is determined by the customer. Through methodology and case studies the book offers insight into how Japanese companies identify customer requirements and describes how to translate customer requirements into qualified quality characteristics, and how to build them into products and services.
ISBN 0-915299-41-0 / 400 pages / $ 75.00 / Order code QFD-BK

## Handbook of Quality Tools
### The Japanese Approach
*edited by Tetsuichi Asaka and Kazuo Ozeki*

The Japanese have stunned the world by their ability to produce top quality products at competitive prices. This comprehensive teaching manual, which includes the 7 traditional and 5 newer QC tools, explains each tool, why it's useful, and how to construct and use it. Information is presented in easy-to-grasp language, with step-by-step instructions, illustrations, and examples of each tool. A perfect training aid, as well as a hands-on reference book, for supervisors, foremen, and/or team leaders. Here's the best resource on the myriad Japanese quality tools changing the face of world manufacturing today. Accessible to everyone in your organization, dealing with both management and shop floor how-to's, you'll find it an indispensable tool in your quest for quality.
ISBN 0-915299-45-3 / 336 pages / $59.95 / Order code HQT-BK

**Productivity Press, Inc., Dept. BK, P.O. Box 3007, Cambridge, MA 02140 1-800-274-9911**

## Winning Ways
### Achieving Zero-Defect Service

*by Jacques Horovitz*

Building a quality service program is essential these days, especially when you consider the high cost of low quality service. This book teaches the service manager how to launch a quality service program and covers techniques for measuring and delivering high standard quality service, ways to detect and eliminate errors, and methods for measuring customer satisfaction. With self-diagnostic questions at the end of each chapter, this simple but thorough how-to book will inspire and lead you to improved customer service performance.
ISBN 0-915299-78-X / 176 pages / $24.95 / Order code WWAYS-BK

## TQC Wisdom of Japan
### Managing for Total Quality Control

*by Hajime Karatsu, translated by David J. Lu*

As productivity goes up, the cost of quality comes down. And as quality improves, the cost to produce comes down. Karatsu, winner of a Deming Prize who has been involved with the quality movement in Japan since its inception, discusses the purpose and techniques of Total Quality Control (TQC), how it differs from QC, and why it is so effective. There is no better introduction to TQC than this book; essential reading for all American managers.
ISBN 0-915299-18-6 / 136 pages / $34.95 / Order code WISD-BK

## Performance Measurement for World Class Manufacturing
### A Model for American Companies

*by Brian H. Maskell*

If your company is adopting world class manufacturing techniques, you'll need new methods of performance measurement to control production variables. In practical terms, this book describes the new methods of performance measurement and how they are used in a changing environment. For manufacturing managers as well as cost accountants, it provides a theoretical foundation of these innovative methods supported by extensive practical examples. The book specifically addresses performance measures for delivery, process time, production flexibility, quality, and finance.
ISBN 0-915299-99-2 / 272 pages / $45.00 / Order code PERFM-BK

## Management for Quality Improvement
### The 7 New QC Tools

*edited by Shigeru Mizuno*

Building on the traditional seven QC tools, these new tools were developed specifically for managers. They help in planning, troubleshooting, and communicating with maximum effectiveness at every stage of a quality improvement program. Just recently made available in the U.S., they are certain to advance quality improvement efforts for anyone involved in project management, quality assurance, MIS, or TQC.
ISBN 0-915299-29-1 / 324 pages / $59.95 / Order code 7QC-BK

**Productivity Press, Inc., Dept. BK, P.O. Box 3007, Cambridge, MA 02140 1-800-274-9911**

# Poka-Yoke
## Improving Product Quality by Preventing Defects

*compiled by Nikkan Kogyo Shimbun, Ltd./Factory Magazine (ed.)*

*preface by Shigeo Shingo*

If your goal is 100% zero defects, here is the book for you — a completely illustrated guide to poka-yoke (mistake-proofing) for supervisors and shop-floor workers. Many poka-yoke devices come from line workers and are implemented with the help of engineering staff. The result is better product quality—and greater participation by workers in efforts to improve your processes, your products, and your company as a whole.
ISBN 0-915299-31-3 / 288 pages / $59.95 / Order code IPOKA-BK

# Achieving Total Quality Management
## A Program for Action

*by Michel Perigord*

This is an outstanding book on total quality management TQM) — a compact guide to the concepts, methods, and techniques involved in achieving total quality. It shows you how to make TQM a company-wide strategy, not just in technical areas, but in marketing and administration as well. Written in an accessible, instructive style by a top European quality expert, it is methodical, logical, and thorough. A historical outline and discussion of the quality-price relationship, is followed by an investigation of the five quality imperatives (conformity, prevention, excellence, measurement, and responsibility). Major methods and tools for total quality are spelled out and implementation strategies are reviewed.
ISBN 0-915299-60-7 / 384 pages / $45.00 / Order Code ACHTQM-BK

# Zero Quality Control
## Source Inspection and the Poka-yoke System

*by Shigeo Shingo, translated by Andrew P. Dillon*

A remarkable combination of source inspection (to detect errors before they become defects) and mistake-proofing devices (to weed out defects before they can be passed down the production line) eliminates the need for statistical quality control. Shingo shows how this proven system for reducing defects to zero turns out the highest quality products in the shortest period of time. With over 100 specific examples illustrated. (Audio-visual training program also available.)
ISBN 0-915299-07-0 / 328 pages / $70.00 / Order code ZQC-BK

# The Poka-Yoke System

*by Shigeo Shingo, translated by Andrew P. Dillon*

Shingo shows how to implement Zero Quality Control (ZQC) on the production line with a combination of source inspection and mistake-proofing devices in this two-part program. Part I explains the theory and concepts and Part II shows practical applications. Package includes facilitator's guides with worksheets, and is available in either slide or video format (please specify when ordering). Each part is approximately 25 minutes long.
235 Slides / ISBN 0-915299-13-5 / $749.00 / Order code S6-BK 2 Videos / ISBN 0-915299-28-3 / $749.00 / Order code V6-BK

**Productivity Press, Inc., Dept. BK, P.O. Box 3007, Cambridge, MA 02140  1-800-274-9911**

**TO ORDER:** Write, phone, or fax Productivity Press, Dept. BK, P.O. Box 3007, Cambridge, MA 02140, phone 1-800-274-9911, fax 1-617-864-6286. Send check or charge to your credit card (American Express, Visa, MasterCard accepted).

**U.S. ORDERS:** Add $5 shipping for first book, $2 each additional for UPS surface delivery. Add $5 for each AV program containing 1 or 2 two tapes; add $12 for each AV program containing 3 or more tapes. CT residents add 8% and MA residents 5% sales tax. We offer attractive quantity discounts for bulk purchases of individual titles; call for more information.

**INTERNATIONAL ORDERS:** Write, phone, or fax for quote and indicate shipping method esired. Pre-payment in U.S. dollars must accompany your order (checks must be drawn on U.S. banks). When quote is returned with payment, your order will be shipped promptly by the method requested.

**NOTE:** Prices are subject to change without notice.

Productivity Press, Inc., Dept. BK, P.O. Box 3007, Cambridge, MA 02140 Telephone: 1-800-274-9911 Fax: 1-617-864-6286

## COMPLETE LIST OF TITLES FROM PRODUCTIVITY PRESS

Akao, Yoji (ed.). **Quality Function Deployment: Integrating Customer Requirements into Product Design**
ISBN 0-915299-41-0 / 1990/ 387 pages / $ 75.00 / order code QFD

Asaka, Tetsuichi and Kazuo Ozeki (eds.). **Handbook of Quality Tools: The Japanese Approach**
ISBN 0-915299-45-3 / 1990 / 336 pages / $59.95 / order code HQT

Belohlav, James A. **Championship Management: An Action Model for High Performance**
ISBN 0-915299-76-3 / 1990 / 265 pages / $29.95 / order code CHAMPS

Birkholz, Charles and Jim Villella. **The Battle to Stay Competitive: Changing the Traditional Workplace**
ISBN 0-915-299-96-8/ 1991 / 110 pages / $9.95 /order code BATTLE

Christopher, William F. **Productivity Measurement Handbook**
ISBN 0-915299-05-4 / 1985 / 680 pages / $137.95 / order code PMH

D'Egidio, Franco. **The Service Era: Leadership in a Global Environment**
ISBN 0-915299-68-2 / 1990 / 165 pages / $29.95 / order code SERA

Ford, Henry. **Today and Tomorrow**
ISBN 0-915299-36-4 / 1988 / 286 pages / $24.95 / order code FORD

Fukuda, Ryuji. **CEDAC: A Tool for Continuous Systematic Improvement**
ISBN 0-915299-26-7 / 1990 / 144 pages / $49.95 / order code CEDAC

Fukuda, Ryuji. **Managerial Engineering: Techniques for Improving Quality and Productivity in the Workplace** (rev.)
ISBN 0-915299-09-7 / 1986 / 208 pages / $39.95 / order code ME

Hatakeyama, Yoshio. **Manager Revolution! A Guide to Survival in Today's Changing Workplace**
ISBN 0-915299-10-0 / 1986 / 208 pages / $24.95 / order code MREV

Hirano, Hiroyuki. **JIT Factory Revolution: A Pictorial Guide to Factory Design of the Future**
ISBN 0-915299-44-5 / 1989 / 227 pages / $49.95 / order code JITFAC

Hirano, Hiroyuki. **JIT Implementation Manual: The Complete Guide to Just-In-Time Manufacturing**
ISBN 0-915299-66-6 / 1990 / 1006 pages / $2500.00 / order code HIRANO

Horovitz, Jacques. **Winning Ways: Achieving Zero-Defect Service**
ISBN 0-915299-78-X / 1990 / 165 pages / $24.95 / order code WWAYS

Japan Human Relations Association (ed.). **The Idea Book: Improvement Through TEI (Total Employee Involvement)**
ISBN 0-915299-22-4 / 1988 / 232 pages / $49.95 / order code IDEA

Japan Human Relations Association (ed.). **The Service Industry Idea Book: Employee Involvement in Retail and Office Improvement**
ISBN 0-915299-65-8 / 1990 / 294 pages / $49.95 / order code SIDEA

Japan Management Association (ed.). **Kanban and Just-In-Time at Toyota: Management Begins at the Workplace** (rev.), Translated by David J. Lu
ISBN 0-915299-48-8 / 1989 / 224 pages / $36.50 / order code KAN

**Productivity Press, Inc., Dept. BK, P.O. Box 3007, Cambridge, MA 02140  1-800-274-9911**

Japan Management Association and Constance E. Dyer. **The Canon Production System: Creative Involvement of the Total Workforce**
ISBN 0-915299-06-2 / 1987 / 251 pages / $36.95 / order code CAN

Jones, Karen (ed.). **The Best of TEI: Current Perspectives on Total Employee Involvement**
ISBN 0-915299-63-1 / 1989 / 502 pages / $175.00 / order code TEI

Kanatsu, Takashi. **TQC for Accounting: A New Role in Companywide Improvement**
ISBN 0-915299-73-9 / 1991 / 244 / $45.00 / order code TQCA

Karatsu, Hajime. **Tough Words For American Industry**
ISBN 0-915299-25-9 / 1988 / 178 pages / $24.95 / order code TOUGH

Karatsu, Hajime. **TQC Wisdom of Japan: Managing for Total Quality Control**, Translated by David J. Lu
ISBN 0-915299-18-6 / 1988 / 136 pages / $34.95 / order code WISD

Kobayashi, Iwao. **20 Keys to Workplace Improvement**
ISBN 0-915299-61-5 / 1990 / 264 pages / $34.95 / order code 20KEYS

Lu, David J. **Inside Corporate Japan: The Art of Fumble-Free Management**
ISBN 0-915299-16-X / 1987 / 278 pages / $24.95 / order code ICJ

Merli, Giorgio. **Total Manufacturing Management: Production Organization for the 1990s**
ISBN 0-915299-58-5 / 1990 / 224 pages / $39.95 / order code TMM

Mizuno, Shigeru (ed.). **Management for Quality Improvement: The 7 New QC Tools**
ISBN 0-915299-29-1 / 1988 / 324 pages / $59.95 / order code 7QC

Monden, Yasuhiro and Michiharu Sakurai (eds.). **Japanese Management Accounting: A World Class Approach to Profit Management**
ISBN 0-915299-50-X / 1990 / 568 pages / $59.95 / order code JMACT

Nachi-Fujikoshi (ed.). **Training for TPM: A Manufacturing Success Story**
ISBN 0-915299-34-8 / 1990 / 272 pages / $59.95 / order code CTPM

Nakajima, Seiichi. **Introduction to TPM: Total Productive Maintenance**
ISBN 0-915299-23-2 / 1988 / 149 pages / $39.95 / order code ITPM

Nakajima, Seiichi. **TPM Development Program: Implementing Total Productive Maintenance**
ISBN 0-915299-37-2 / 1989 / 428 pages / $85.00 / order code DTPM

Nikkan Kogyo Shimbun, Ltd./Factory Magazine (ed.). **Poka-yoke: Improving Product Quality by Preventing Defects**
ISBN 0-915299-31-3 / 1989 / 288 pages / $59.95 / order code IPOKA

Ohno, Taiichi. **Toyota Production System: Beyond Large-Scale Production**
ISBN 0-915299-14-3 / 1988 / 162 pages / $39.95 / order code OTPS

Ohno, Taiichi. **Workplace Management**
ISBN 0-915299-19-4 / 1988 / 165 pages / $34.95 / order code WPM

Ohno, Taiichi and Setsuo Mito. **Just-In-Time for Today and Tomorrow**
ISBN 0-915299-20-8 / 1988 / 208 pages / $34.95 / order code OMJIT

Perigord, Michel. **Achieving Total Quality Management: A Program for Action**
ISBN 0-915299-60-7 / 1991 / 384 pages / $45.00 / order code ACHTQM

**Productivity Press, Inc., Dept. BK, P.O. Box 3007, Cambridge, MA 02140  1-800-274-9911**

Psarouthakis, John. **Better Makes Us Best**
ISBN 0-915299-56-9 / 1989 / 112 pages / $16.95 / order code BMUB

Robson, Ross (ed.). **The Quality and Productivity Equation: American Corporate Strategies for the 1990s**
ISBN 0-915299-71-2 / 1990 / 558 pages / $29.95 / order code QPE

Shetty, Y.K and Vernon M. Buehler (eds.). **Competing Through Productivity and Quality**
ISBN 0-915299-43-7 / 1989 / 576 pages / $39.95 / order code COMP

Shingo, Shigeo. **Non-Stock Production: The Shingo System for Continuous Improvement**
ISBN 0-915299-30-5 / 1988 / 480 pages / $75.00 / order code NON

Shingo, Shigeo. **A Revolution In Manufacturing: The SMED System**, Translated by Andrew P. Dillon
ISBN 0-915299-03-8 / 1985 / 383 pages / $70.00 / order code SMED

Shingo, Shigeo. **The Sayings of Shigeo Shingo: Key Strategies for Plant Improvement**, Translated by Andrew P. Dillon
ISBN 0-915299-15-1 / 1987 / 208 pages / $39.95 / order code SAY

Shingo, Shigeo. **A Study of the Toyota Production System from an Industrial Engineering Viewpoint** (rev.)
ISBN 0-915299-17-8 / 1989 / 293 pages / $39.95 / order code STREV

Shingo, Shigeo. **Zero Quality Control: Source Inspection and the Poka-yoke System**, Translated by Andrew P. Dillon
ISBN 0-915299-07-0 / 1986 / 328 pages / $70.00 / order code ZQC

Shinohara, Isao (ed.). **New Production System: JIT Crossing Industry Boundaries**
ISBN 0-915299-21-6 / 1988 / 224 pages / $34.95 / order code NPS

Sugiyama, Tomo. **The Improvement Book: Creating the Problem-Free Workplace**
ISBN 0-915299-47-X / 1989 / 236 pages / $49.95 / order code IB

Suzue, Toshio and Akira Kohdate. **Variety Reduction Program (VRP): A Production Strategy for Product Diversification**
ISBN 0-915299-32-1 / 1990 / 164 pages / $59.95 / order code VRP

Tateisi, Kazuma. **The Eternal Venture Spirit: An Executive's Practical Philosophy**
ISBN 0-915299-55-0 / 1989 / 208 pages/ $19.95 / order code EVS

Yasuda, Yuzo. **40 Years, 20 Million Ideas: The Toyota Suggestion System**
ISBN 0-915299-74-7 / 1991 / 210 pages / 39.95 / order code 4020

Productivity Press, Inc., Dept. BK, P.O. Box 3007, Cambridge, MA 02140 1-800-274-9911

## Audio-Visual Programs

Japan Management Association. **Total Productive Maintenance:
Maximizing Productivity and Quality**
ISBN 0-915299-46-1 / 167 slides / 1989 / $749.00 / order code STPM
ISBN 0-915299-49-6 / 2 videos / 1989 / $749.00 / order code VTPM

Shingo, Shigeo. **The SMED System**, Translated by Andrew P. Dillon
ISBN 0-915299-11-9 / 181 slides / 1986 / $749.00 / order code S5
ISBN 0-915299-27-5 / 2 videos / 1987 / $749.00 / order code V5

Shingo, Shigeo. **The Poka-yoke System**, Translated by Andrew P. Dillon
ISBN 0-915299-13-5 / 235 slides / 1987 / $749.00 / order code S6
ISBN 0-915299-28-3 / 2 videos / 1987 / $749.00 / order code V6

Returns of AV programs willl be accepted for incorrect or damaged
shipments only.

**TO ORDER:** Write, phone, or fax Productivity Press, Dept. BK, P.O. Box 3007, Cambridge, MA 02140, phone 1-800-274-9911, fax 617-864-6286. Send check or charge to
your credit card (American Express, Visa, MasterCard accepted).

**U.S. ORDERS:** Add $5 shipping for first book, $2 each additional for UPS surface
delivery. CT residents add 8% and MA residents 5% sales tax. For each AV program that
you order, add $5 for programs with 1 or 2 tapes, and $12 for programs with 3 or more
tapes.

**INTERNATIONAL ORDERS:** Write, phone, or fax for quote and indicate shipping method
desired.  Pre-payment in U.S. dollars must accompany your order (checks must be